Justice Provocateur

JUSTICE PROVOCATEUR

Jane Tennison and Policing
in *Prime Suspect*

GRAY CAVENDER
AND NANCY C. JURIK

University of Illinois Press
URBANA, CHICAGO, AND SPRINGFIELD

All photographs courtesy of Granada Television/
ITV/Rex USA unless noted otherwise.

Library of Congress Cataloging-in-Publication Data
Cavender, Gray, 1947–
Justice provocateur : Jane Tennison and policing
in Prime suspect /
Gray Cavender and Nancy C. Jurik.
p.   cm.
Includes bibliographical references and index.
ISBN 978-0-252-03719-1 (hard cover : acid-free paper) —
ISBN 978-0-252-07870-5 (pbk. : acid-free paper) —
ISBN 978-0-252-09431-6 (e-book)
1. Prime suspect (Television program)
2. Women on television. 3. Sex role on television.
4. Television cop shows—Great Britain—History and criticism.
I. Jurik, Nancy C. II. Title.
PN1992.77.P67C38   2012
791.45'72—dc23   2011052788

Contents

Acknowledgments

We are grateful to ITV/Granada Productions and Rex USA for granting us permission to use their *Prime Suspect* images in this book. However, none of the contents of this publication is intended to imply that it is endorsed by the program's broadcasters or production companies involved. We appreciate technical assistance from Kevan Mitton and the Film and Media Studies Lab at Arizona State University. We also thank colleagues who have helped us in so many ways during our work on the *Prime Suspect* series: Madelaine Adelman, Jane Aiken, David Altheide, Aaron Baker, Jennifer Brown, Susan Caringella, Anne Catalano, Rebecca Dobash, Russell Dobash, Jeffrey Dunne, Gabriel Garcia-Merritt, Crystal Griffith, Frances Heidensohn, Drew Humphries, Deborah Jermyn, Paul Knepper, Eric Margolis, Linda Mizejewski, Elsie Moore, Mary Romero, Tim Rowlands, Elizabeth Stanko, Marjorie Zatz, and UIP reviewers and staff. We also want to thank the students of Jurik's fall 2010 Women and Work course and Cavender's spring 2011 Justice and the Media course for their insights regarding *Prime Suspect*, *The Closer*, and *The Wire*. Several women police officers and administrators at the London Metropolitan Police were kind enough to speak with Nancy Jurik about their work experiences, work/life balance, and views of media images such as those in *Prime Suspect*. Of course, the analysis and arguments offered in the book are our own. We are equal coauthors of this book.

Introduction

Prime Suspect (Granada Television) is one of the most popular British television exports to the United States and around the globe. The series chronicles the career and personal life of Jane Tennison, initially a detective chief inspector (DCI) and later a detective superintendent (DS) for the London Metropolitan Police. Dame Helen Mirren plays Tennison, a woman officer who solves tough cases that expose complex social injustices, all the while fighting her way up the ranks of the male-dominated organization of British policing. In one *Prime Suspect* episode, her dad characterizes Tennison's passionate pursuit of justice:

> You know, up until the age of twelve you were an angel. You'd light up a room, and then bang—overnight you were a teenager. You ran us ragged, and it got worse, into this, into that, so certain, so bloody-minded, you couldn't leave anything alone. You terrified me, but you know what? I didn't mind, I was so proud. You had convictions. Well, I buried mine at that [concentration] camp. All I wanted was your mother, a steady job, children, and nothing to do with the evil I saw at that camp. But here you are, having to deal with it again. But you will. You will. You know what's right, and you'll do it.

There have been seven *Prime Suspect* installments. Each episode runs approximately three to four hours, allowing for in-depth character and plot development. The first episode, *Prime Suspect 1*, aired in 1991 in the United Kingdom on ITV1 on two successive nights and in 1992 in the United States in weekly installments that lasted a month. The seventh and last episode,

Prime Suspect 7: The Final Act, aired in 2006 in the UK and in 2007 in the United States. With more than fourteen million viewers in the UK alone, *Prime Suspect* was ranked first place in popular British Television Channel 4's "Top 10 TV Cops" (Jermyn 2003, 61). In the United States the programs were broadcast on the Public Broadcasting System (PBS) series *Mystery!* and indeed *Prime Suspect* has been the most popular film series in *Mystery!* program history. It was so popular that PBS relocated *Prime Suspect* to its flagship venue, *Masterpiece Theater*, for some of the episodes. A US version of the series premiered in the fall of 2011 on NBC network television. The rights for distribution of this US version were sold to several countries, but the fate of the series for spring 2012 is still uncertain due to low audience ratings.

Critical acclaim for *Prime Suspect* and leading actress Dame Helen Mirren has been abundant. With regard to *Prime Suspect 6*, the British news-

Jane Tennison in
Prime Suspect is played
by Helen Mirren.

paper the *Observer* wrote: "*Prime Suspect 6* . . . [is] the very rarest sort of television . . ., one of the most worthwhile TV experiences of the year and Mirren is, basically, a goddess" (Flett 2003). Tom Shales of the *Washington Post* described *Prime Suspect 3* as "grippingly suspenseful from the get-go . . ., one of the most absorbing, well-acted, and mercilessly nervewracking dramas. . . . Sensational would not be too strong a word" (1994). A critic with the *New York Times* wrote about *Prime Suspect 5*: "Here is a performance that will loom large in television history books" (O'Connor 1997). *Prime Suspect* is a global phenomenon. The episodes have aired in seventy-eight countries, and worldwide audiences for some episodes have approached two hundred million viewers (commentary from *Prime Suspect 6* DVD). The series has won more than twenty-three international awards (Hallam 2005, 64). These have included British Academy of Film and Television Arts (BAFTA) awards for best drama serial and best television actress for Mirren, US Emmys for outstanding miniseries and outstanding actress for Mirren, Edgar Allan Poe Awards for best television feature or miniseries, Peabody Awards, and the Television Critics Association Award for Outstanding Achievement in a Miniseries or Special.

Prime Suspect's significance goes well beyond its popularity, however. The series is pathbreaking because it centers a strong woman lead in a gritty portrayal within what had been an otherwise overwhelmingly male-dominated police procedural subgenre. Moreover, beyond its significance in terms of gender imagery, *Prime Suspect* has shaped the police procedural subgenre by setting higher standards for conveying a sense of social realism in the coverage of police work and, more specifically, what media analysts call "forensic realism" (Jermyn 2003; Deutsch and Cavender 2008). Its impact can be seen in other successful television crime programs in the UK, including *Silent Witness* (1996–) and *M.I.T.: Murder Investigation Team* (2003–5), and in the United States, including *The Closer* (2005–) and *Crime Scene Investigation* (*CSI*) (2000–).

We argue in this book that the series is also significant with regard to its treatment of contemporary social problems and messages about justice. *Prime Suspect* episodes make visible the societal roots of complex social problems and the experiences of socially marginalized individuals who are victimized. Tennison's exploits take viewers to worlds they might never see and expose them to the lives of individuals who might otherwise be invisible to many middle-class and elite peoples of the world. Tennison's responses to these situations are not without problems; she is clearly no superhero. However, her efforts to bring justice to socially marginalized victims offer the opportunity for viewers, students, and scholars alike to reflect on complicated issues of justice in ways that go beyond the standard law-and-order approach of most works in the television crime genre generally and the police procedural drama in particular.

Giving visibility to the experiences of the socially marginalized and providing an expanded treatment of justice are important for even fictional portraits because they help individuals to better imagine more just societies. The mass media are a central vehicle for dissemination of culturally dominant views of gender, race, and other dimensions of social identities. They are also important conveyors of impressions about social problems and just solutions to them. Nevertheless, most crime genre fiction negatively stereotypes the socially marginalized and favors a shallow sense of justice—one that focuses narrowly on actions of the criminal justice system and on remedies that reproduce a conservative view of social order (Knight 1980, 4; Lenz 2003).

As individuals who are concerned about social justice and who recognize the importance of media in shaping public perceptions and generating discussions about social problems, we want to identify cultural productions that promote contemplation of fairness, equality, and justice. Toward this end, we have developed an ideal type model of progressive moral fiction in order to better highlight cultural productions that offer insights into the lived experiences of socially marginalized individuals and locate them within a larger societal context of inequality and oppression; at the same time, we want to portray individuals or groups who work to transform unjust social arrangements and promote social justice. We intend to utilize this model as a heuristic for analyzing the *Prime Suspect* series and other media productions to generate public and classroom debates about social justice issues.

We will argue that the *Prime Suspect* series provides glimpses of a deeper sense of justice that reveal oppressive social structures and social inequalities that are reproduced in and by the criminal justice system. Some sources argue that it is the women-centered nature of the series that leads to such socially relevant narratives (Mizejewski 2004).

Still, not all critics and scholars agree that *Prime Suspect* is truly transformative of either television or the crime genre. Several critics argue that it is actually more subversive of transformation efforts than a radical departure from business as usual. They argue that the Tennison character and series as a whole mostly reinforce the oppressive nature of television and the crime genre to women and other socially marginalized individuals and further reinforce the legitimacy of oppressive law enforcement and legal structures in society (Brooks 1994; Tomc 1995).

In order to begin to assess these arguments, it is necessary to present a brief history of the crime genre and women's place in it as well as a brief history of how television has portrayed women more generally. To a degree, television's increasing depiction of women, especially in the workplace, parallels the progress of real women in the workplace.

The Crime Genre

The crime genre has enjoyed a long-running popularity across media: short stories and novels, plays, films, radio, television, and now video games. A genre is a taxonomy of cultural production; genres are defined by certain recurring elements. The crime genre is defined by the expectation that a crime occurs and that a detective discovers the culprits and brings them to justice. One of the earliest examples of the crime genre in popular culture is *The Newgate Calendar*. First published in London in 1773, *The Newgate Calendar* exemplified two features that came to be commonplace in the crime genre. There was a moral component of *The Newgate Calendar* in that it contained stories of people who had turned to crime but, by the end of the story, often realized the error of their ways and were in a sense redeemed. *The Newgate Calendar* also purported to present true stories of real people. Notions of realism—either stories based on real cases or a presentational style that seeks to generate a sense of verisimilitude—characterize many of the productions in the crime genre.

Many commentators credit Edgar Allan Poe as being the creator of the modern detective story. In short stories such as "The Murders in the Rue Morgue" (1841) and "The Purloined Letter" (1845), Poe introduced the character of the detective, C. Auguste Dupin, who uses ratiocination as a method of investigation. One of Poe's detective short stories, "The Mystery of Marie Rogêt" (1842), also exhibits a tendency toward realism. The story was a fictionalized account of an actual unsolved murder, that of Mary Rogers in New York City, and Poe promised that his fictional detective would solve it.

More than thirty years after Poe's work, Sir Arthur Conan Doyle created a similar detective, Sherlock Holmes, who would become one of the most enduring characters in Western literature. Between 1874 and 1914 Conan Doyle produced fifty-six short stories and four novels featuring Holmes, and the character has appeared in countless radio programs, films, television series, and plays. Even today there is a cottage industry in "recently discovered" manuscripts that continue the exploits of Holmes and his companion, Dr. Watson. These contemporary novels and films pair Holmes with other actual or fictional historical figures such as Sigmund Freud (*The Seven Percent Solution*) and Jack the Ripper (*Murder by Decree*). The continuing popularity of the character is reflected in *Sherlock Holmes*, a 2009 film that turns Holmes and Watson into action heroes, and a current television series, *Sherlock* (BBC Wales and WGBH Boston), that locates Holmes and Watson in contemporary London.

In the 1930s the crime genre gained popularity in the United States in a greatly altered form with detectives in the "hard-boiled" tradition. Appearing in pulp magazines such as the *Black Mask*, these stories also featured private detectives, but these were grittier and more violent stories than those of Holmes or other detectives such as Miss Marple, Hercule Poirot, and Lord Peter Wimsey. Dashiell Hammett, one of the best-known writers in the hard-boiled tradition, created Sam Spade, a hard-drinking private detective who used his fists as well as his wits. Hammett's narrative style, including his close attention to detail and description, continued the genre's realist tradition. The popularity of Hammett and his contemporaries generated films that were based on the short stories and novels of the hard-boiled writers. As we will discuss in later chapters, these stories and films were often critical of the existing power structure, including the police. The films in this style came to be known as film noir, a name that reflected both the bleakness of their worldview and their aesthetic presentation, which included a cinematography that privileged dark, shadowy productions (Cavender and Jurik 1998).

Ironically, at the same time that these hard-boiled and noir productions were appearing, there also appeared another crime subgenre, the police procedural. Police procedural stories, radio dramas, and films featured not alienated private detectives but hard-working police officers or other government agents. The police organization was the star of these productions, and they gave a behind-the-scenes view of the police and their routines. The narratives sometimes were based on actual cases or newspaper accounts of crimes, which gave them the sense of realism that we have mentioned. Some of the films (*Panic in the Streets*, 1950; *The Naked City*, 1948) were shot in a documentary style that further enhanced their realism. In part, this style drew upon the movie newsreels that were popular during World War II (Krutnik 1991; Wilson 2000). This style was adopted in 1950s UK television police series such as *Fabian of the Yard* (1954–56) and *Dixon of Dock Green* (1955–76). Sydney-Smith (2007) attributes this style of television crime drama to the influence of writers from the BBC's documentary unit. It is also associated with British social realism television, a popular style that by the 1960s sought to portray the lives and issues of real, common people.

Dragnet (1951–59) and *Highway Patrol* (1955–59) were popular US television police procedural series. Jack Webb, the creator and star of *Dragnet*, was a stickler for police realism, and he employed documentary-style production techniques, including location shooting and characters whose terse, clipped delivery was laced with police jargon. Webb rode on patrol with officers and even attended the Police Academy, all in the interests of enhancing the program's sense of realism (Dunning 1998). *Dragnet* also aired in the UK. Most of these 1950s police programs in the United States and UK presented a comforting message to viewers that their problems were important and that police were heroes who protected them.

In the 1960s this message changed with UK police programs such as *Z Cars* (1962–78) that offered a faster pace with more frequent incidents of street violence. The message of *Z Cars* was far less reassuring than that of 1950s British police programs. Earlier episodes of *Z Cars* addressed issues of police corruption and violence, but after complaints from British police officials, later episodes toned down implicit critiques of the police organization. US programs such as *The Mod Squad* (1968–73) and *Ironside* (1967–75) began to engage more liberal values and to acknowledge problems of social marginalization and corrupting forces within the police organization (Cooke 2003). Both programs featured women and members of racial/ethnic populations as prominent characters. *Dragnet* (1967–70) reappeared in the United States and continued its documentary style but added an increased moralistic tone to its narration by star Jack Webb, a tone that was critical of the 1960s counterculture. Webb also created the US police drama *Adam 12* (1968–75), a program that featured conflicts and dilemmas faced by police. Its procedures were viewed as so realistic that the program was used in real police training academies. Other US television police dramas in the 1960s used various techniques to evoke a sense of realism. *The FBI* (1965–74) featured stories drawn from actual cases, and at the end of each episode fugitives who were wanted by the FBI were presented. Even so, the agents in the series offered a more glamorized portrait of police work than did the police officers in *Dragnet*.

Notwithstanding the popularity of the police procedural, private detectives and criminal defense attorneys were also television fixtures in the late 1950s and 1960s, for example, *77 Sunset Strip* (1958–64), *Bourbon Street Beat* (1959–60), and *Surfside 6* (1960–62). The stars of these series were almost always attractive men, and their cases were typically more exciting than realistic portraits of real-life private detectives. Television dramas featuring criminal defense attorneys also were popular in the 1960s, including *Perry Mason* (1957–66), which is perhaps the best-known lawyer series of all time. The character was based on a successful series of lawyer/crime novels. The novels and the television series were whodunits in which Perry Mason revealed the identity of the real killer (never his client) in a closing courtroom scene. Other lawyer programs deemphasized the whodunit in favor of social problems. *The Defenders* (1961–65) featured defense attorneys who undertook criminal cases that involved social issues such as the death penalty and pornography. Similarly, the criminal defense attorneys in *The Bold Ones* (1968–72) handled cases that touched on contemporary social issues; for example, in one episode a member of the Black Panthers was charged with the murder of a white cop.

Attention again shifted during the 1970s. Films such as *Dirty Harry* (1971) and television programs such as *Police Story* (1973–78) in the United States and *The Sweeney* (1975–78) in the UK ushered in a new era of programming that maintained interest in police routines but accentuated iconoclastic police heroes. Many of these programs were tough portraits of crime-ridden urban settings but tended to reveal a less positive view of the police. *Police Story* focused on mundane police routines but also dealt with problems such as police corruption, racism, and resulting tensions with ethnic communities. The personal lives of characters were also addressed. *The Sweeney* (named after the Cockney nickname for the British police special investigation division called the Flying Squad) featured a fast-paced drama that showed bursts of violence by police against street criminals. Although *The*

Sweeney and programs like it continued to mimic a documentary realist style, these action-packed episodes contrast with the slow pace and routine nature of their predecessors and indeed of police work. This type of program creates a fantasy sense of realism (Sydney-Smith 2007).

Another strand of 1970s police dramas featured quirky individual police officers such as *Columbo* (1971–78), *McCloud* (1970–77), *Kojak* (1973–78), and *Baretta* (1975–78) who exhibited their own special idiosyncrasies, sometimes skirted the rulebook, and sought to bring about their own unconventional and sometimes "higher" form of justice. For example, Baretta was an undercover officer who often blurred the line between the police and the criminal.

From the 1980s until the present, the private detective has been virtually displaced on television in the United States with successful police dramas such as the hit series *Hill Street Blues* (1981–87). *Hill Street Blues* set more rigorous standards for realism that are still emulated by more recent police series such as *NYPD Blue* (1993–2005) and *Law & Order* (1990–2010). For example, in *Hill Street Blues* even the sound production—the placement of microphones and actors who generated a background dialogue—was designed to generate the "feel" of a real squad room (Gitlin 1983). One of the longest-running UK television series, *The Bill* (1984–2010), also featured police routines. Occasionally, *The Bill* even parodied US police dramas like *Hill Street Blues*. Some episodes of *The Bill* opened in the same manner as *Hill Street Blues*, with the officers at roll call receiving updates on crime issues in their beat. Occasionally, the officer conducting the briefing even delivered the line of dialogue popularized by the briefing sergeant in *Hill Street Blues*: "Be careful out there." At other times, the cops in *The Bill* jokingly reference police jargon popularized in US television series. Women were present in these police ensemble casts, but their roles were largely subordinated to the men series stars. UK television has preserved the private detective more so than in the United States.

For many decades, women fared badly in the television crime genre and the police procedural genre in particular. Series were male-dominated, and women were either invisible or featured in traditionally feminine roles. There were occasional exceptions to these patterns in the 1960s and 1970s, but more significant challenges did not emerge until the 1980s. To a great extent, the absence of women in police dramas reflected the real world of policing.

The History of Women in Real-World Policing

A review of the history of women in policing suggests that throughout the nineteenth and early twentieth centuries women worked in a narrow range of duties in police organizations. Indeed, before the 1970s nearly all police officers in the UK, the United States, and indeed around the world were men (Brown and Heidensohn 2000; Martin and Jurik 2007). The relatively small numbers of women working in policing were initially relegated to clerical duties and, beginning in the early twentieth century, to cases involving women and child victims and offenders. Germany is believed to have been the first country to hire a woman to work as a police officer in 1905, although this "experiment" was quickly terminated. The UK, the United States, and several other countries also began so-called experimental programs, with women police officers assigned to specialized women's police bureaus and working in social work–like capacities with women and children (Schulz 1995).

The response to women's early twentieth-century entry into policing was less than cordial, and this was reflected in formal administrator proclamations as well as in the popular press (Brown and Heidensohn 2000). Characterizations of women varied from condemnations of policewomen as fragile and incompetent to descriptions of them as overly aggressive and mannish. By the 1950s some acceptance of these female pioneers emerged in the form of claims that properly trained women could perform adequately enough to relieve men of the "feminine chores" that might otherwise distract men from their "more important and masculine" crime-fighting responsibilities. Some official and popular stories challenged earlier descriptions of policewomen as mannish lesbians and instead highlighted their sexual attractiveness. Throughout the 1950s and 1960s the growth in policewomen's numbers was slow, and their integration into many police duties was resisted (Martin and Jurik 2007).

In the 1970s equal opportunity legislation exerted pressure on police departments to assign women to a full range of police duties. In anticipation of equality legislation (i.e., the Sex Discrimination Act of 1975), top British police administrators moved toward gender integration. In the United States, equal opportunity legislation converged with funding policies tied to its implementation and facilitated the movement of women into police patrol positions (i.e., the Crime Control Act of 1973). Despite official policies of equal opportunity, extensive and overt opposition to policewomen continued at all levels in both countries. The integration of women into more aspects of policing was prompted not only by social movement pressures and legislation for equal rights. Changes in the politics of policing over the decades led to pressures for transformations in police organization and cultures (Reiner 1994). Periodic crises in the legitimacy of policing were provoked by highly publicized scandals of police corruption, unlawful police acts of violence, or inadequate crime scene management (Brown and Heidensohn 2000; Martin and Jurik 2007). Charges of police corruption had also fueled the development of the specialized women's police bureaus in the early 1900s. The women's bureaus attracted more highly educated and middle-class recruits than did men's police units. As upstanding young women, these policewomen were viewed as less corruption-prone and more professional than their men counterparts. Policewomen were also viewed as particularly skilled at working with women and children (Schulz 1995).

Over time, interest in the all-women's police bureaus waned, and women's duties continued but in limited capacities. Crises in policing during the 1960s and 1970s prompted a renewed interest in the inclusion of more men of color and more women as police officers. During the 1960s many police responded to civil rights and anti–Vietnam War protesters with what would be later deemed excessive force. Such events led to special investigative commissions at national and local levels and mandates for the increased implementation of more professionalized police training, community policing programs, and a more responsive and caring police ethos. In such initiatives, equal opportunities and increased diversity of police forces figured prominently (Brown and Heidensohn 2000, 96; Jurik and Martin 2001). It was believed by many calling for police and other criminal justice reforms that adding in more men of color and women of all races would result in a more culturally sensitive and communicative police force that would be able to diffuse rather than escalate community protest and conflict (Martin and Jurik 2007).

Thus, pressures from social movements (e.g., women's rights, civil rights, gay rights), legislative shifts (e.g., equal opportunity laws), and police legitimacy converged to more fully integrate women into policing. Women's duties and numbers have slowly expanded in UK and US police departments since the 1970s. However, integration policies effectively promoted the end of separate and specialized women's divisions. Research has documented both the advancements of and the barriers faced by women police officers over time (Martin 1980; Morash and Greene 1986; Hunt 1990; Brown and Fielding 1993; Brown 1998, 2007; Brown and Heidensohn 2000; Jurik and Martin 2001). This occupational shift—women moving into the full range of police duties—was eventually reflected in the crime genre as well.

Women, Television, and the Crime Genre

Television is one of our principal contemporary storytellers. Like folklore tales of long ago, it deals in myths that symbolize issues that are important to society. Programs and even genres reflect cultural assumptions and values (Rapping 2003; Wittebols 2004). Television bombards us with images that reflect these cultural values and influence how we see social issues and ourselves (Press 1991; McCullagh 2002). But television is a conservative, profit-driven medium, and to be profitable, programs must lure and hold audiences. To maintain high audience ratings, programs must resonate with dominant cultural constructions and values.

In a sense, television represents a kind of archaeological record. As society changes, as new cultural constructions emerge, television must change if its programs are to be relevant and interesting to the audience. It is for this reason that scholars, especially feminist scholars, analyze the history of television programs. In the 1970s, for example, when the social landscape changed and married middle-class women entered the paid workforce in increasing numbers, television responded with its own programmatic changes. Women characters left the home and, in some cases, the family and entered the workplace (Dow 1996). For example, Mary Tyler Moore costarred in one of the most popular US television comedies during the 1960s, *The Dick Van Dyke Show* (1961–66). She played Laura Petrie, a stay-at-home wife and mother. A decade later, Moore starred in another popular television program, *The Mary Tyler Moore Show* (1970–77). She played Mary Richards, a single career woman who made her way in the workforce. At the same time, however, gender and media scholars such as Bonnie Dow (1996) and Charlotte Brunsdon (2000) note that although television changes with the times, its programmatic changes are still bounded by institutional constraints and genre conventions.

Similar shifts are evident in television's portrayal of women in crime drama over time. The television crime drama was especially resistant to more progressive roles for women. Traditionally, women in lead roles were a rarity in television crime drama (or in crime novels). In the early 1970s, for example, US and UK television offered many police dramas starring male protagonists (e.g., *Adam 12*, *The Sweeney*). Women's roles were highly stereotyped or totally absent from these programs. By the late 1970s, as they entered the real-world occupations of policing, women played increasingly more important roles in television crime dramas. Linda Mizejewski (2004, 11) suggests that at this point women so significantly infiltrated the television crime genre that they were virtually a part of "central casting" in such programming, albeit in limited and stereotyped roles. Women protagonists in crime dramas were stereotypically pretty, and despite some limited accommodations to an equal employment opportunity type of feminism, they were generally subordinated to stronger men characters.

Women actually began to appear as crime genre protagonists on television in the 1960s. *The Avengers* (1961–69), a British spy series that was also a hit in the United States, featured a man/woman team: John Steed (Patrick McNee) and initially Cathy Gale (Honor Blackman). Blackman argued that there was a feminist dimension to the series because of her character's self-assurance and physical prowess (Buxton 1990, 100; also see Sydney-Smith 2009, 49). The Cathy Gale character influenced several later television portraits of women in the crime genre. In the fourth season of *The Avengers*, Blackman was replaced by Diana Rigg, who played the more glamorous but still capable martial arts and fencing expert Mrs. Emma Peel. The name of the character stands for "man appeal" (i.e., "m appeal"), a characteristic that producers viewed to be an essential component of her image (Rogers 1989). Mrs. Peel, who was also a brilliant chemist, rarely lost a fight; she rescued her male partner as often as he rescued her. Like the male-centered police series *The Sweeney*, *The Avengers* was a fantasy-oriented production, but a far more stylized one that importantly featured a woman as a lead character.

Television's first woman private investigator appeared in the US series *Honey West* (1965–66). Honey West (Anne Francis) was influenced by the Cathy Gale character in *The Avengers*. Like *The Avengers*, *Honey West* featured a pretty and sexualized character, but one who was a strong and independent woman. She worked on her own without a male partner. Although the series was short-lived, by the 1970s several other series appeared that centered on either women investigators or women police officers.

Police Woman (1974–78) was one of the first successful television police dramas that featured a woman police officer in the starring role. The series starred popular film actress Angie Dickenson as Pepper Anderson. Like her predecessors, Pepper was "television friendly." She was a woman and the lead character, but she also was glamorous, often in disguise as a prostitute, and she was often saved from danger by her male partner.

The first television program starring a black woman as a police officer also appeared in 1974. *Get Christie Love* (1974) began as a made-for-television film, and this pilot was quickly followed by a television series (1974–75). Teresa Graves played an undercover police detective who was determined to overthrow a drug ring. The character of Christie Love is often associated with popular blaxploitation movies of the 1970s. Christie Love was a hip cop who hit bad guys with her large purses and karate-chopped them into unconsciousness—moves that were toned down in the series. She was known for her confrontational dialogue, such as "I got news for you, Lieutenant—Christie Love isn't a quitter, sugah. She intends to fight!" Like Emma Peel, Honey West, and Pepper Anderson, Christie Love was a glamorous and sexually appealing but strong television character. Her boss, who saw no reason for women in policing, often tried to sideline her by giving her trivial cases, but these usually ended with Christie solving really big crimes. *Get Christie Love* lasted for only one season, perhaps in part because its time slot competed with the very popular *Police Woman*. The series was, nonetheless, significant, first, because a black woman lead character was a rarity in US television in the early 1970s and, second, because the Christie Love character was loosely based on Dorothy Uhnak's series of crime novels published between 1968 and 1970. Uhnak's protagonist, Christie Opara, a white New York City detective, was the first policewoman to be featured in a series of police procedural novels (Dove 1982, 151).

Perhaps the height of the glamorous woman investigators came in *Charlie's Angels* (1976–81). Aaron Spelling, creator of *Honey West*, also developed *Charlie's Angels* (Mizejewski 2004, 55). According to the series' backstory, the three lead characters were initially rookie police officers who now worked for a private investigator: Charlie. *Charlie's Angels* made no pretense of being a police procedural; instead, these young women were pictured in exotic locations, often clad in bikinis, and subservient to the authority of the never-seen-on-screen Charlie. Despite many criticisms of the program, Mizejewski (2004, 69) points out that *Charlie's Angels* offered something very new in television: a women's buddy format.

In both the UK and the United States, television police dramas proliferated in the 1970s and continued to enjoy success in the 1980s. Programs like *Charlie's Angels* were more fantasy than realism, and, increasingly, television police dramas came to be dominated by the police procedural. As noted earlier, women were part of ensemble casts in hit series such as *The Bill* and *Hill Street Blues*. Although these series portrayed women as accepted by their male peers, the atmosphere and plots were typically male-oriented, and women played subordinate and sometimes sexualized roles. Women police had a presence on *Hill Street Blues* but were most frequently shown doing paperwork in the station and rarely out on patrol until later seasons. In *The Bill*, sexualized jokes between men and women officers were portrayed as acceptable and commonplace. In one episode of *Hill Street Blues*, the character Lucille Bates (Betty Thomas) is shown interacting with her sergeant and is relieved when he tells her that he finds her attractive.

Despite the large number of 1980s television series that continued with male-dominated casts and themes, there were several significant police procedural dramas during the 1980s that featured women as lead characters. The programs also began to address, although typically gently, some issues of gender discrimination within policing. In the UK, *The Gentle Touch* and *Juliet Bravo* appeared, and both series predated a highly popular US television police procedural series, *Cagney & Lacey*. *The Gentle Touch* (1980–84) starred Jill Gascoine as DCI Maggie Forbes, who is assigned to the Seven Dials station in London. In the opening episode, DCI Forbes, a career officer with the London Metropolitan Police, tracks her husband's killer; her husband was a police constable. Throughout the series, DCI Forbes investigates a variety of crimes that are often connected to larger social issues (Sydney-Smith 2009). As *The Gentle Touch* addressed such topics, its scripts offered some social commentary. For example, before he is murdered, DCI Forbes's husband indicates that he may resign from the police because changes in British society have altered the nature of policing, and the public no longer respects the police. Although DCI Forbes enjoys the support of her superior, dialogue occasionally suggests that some in the police hierarchy opposed the assignment of a woman DCI. Some citizens also make it clear that they would prefer to work with a policeman, not a policewoman. DCI Forbes's home life and its accompanying tensions were regularly addressed in the series. Issues included the difficulty of being a professional woman who works long, irregular hours and who also is the single mom of a sometimes troublesome teenage son. Sydney-Smith (2009) notes that such personal, noncrime story lines, what Nelsen (1997) calls "soapification," became a standard feature of police procedurals. DCI Forbes considers resigning from the police and is encouraged to do so by her father, but she continues in the job because she enjoys it. As *The Gentle Touch* title suggests, DCI Forbes solves cases but along the way dispenses advice and good sense to the citizens with whom she comes in contact. This trend toward melodrama, a genre formerly associated with women's audiences, gradually became more generally prominent in television primetime programming (Wittebols 2004).

The second important series, *Juliet Bravo* (1980–85), aired only four months after *The Gentle Touch*. Ian Kennedy Martin, who had worked on *The Sweeney*, created *Juliet Bravo* and wrote a number of its scripts. In the early years of the series, Inspector Jean Darblay (Stephanie Turner) heads a police station in Hartley, a fictional town in Lancashire. A penchant for documentary-like realism is apparent in the series: Martin based Darblay on a model policewoman. Also, consistent with the procedural subgenre, plots tended to focus more on police routines than on serious crime (Sydney-Smith 2009, 51). The less-than-urban nature of the setting also resulted in some plotlines that portrayed the criminals and the police in a humorous manner. Inspector Darblay experiences sexist resentment from citizens and her subordinates, and this disrespect is more pronounced than the sexism that DCI Maggie Forbes typically experienced in *The Gentle Touch*. In the early episodes, Inspector Darblay's subordinates often encourage her to await her male superior's arrival on the scene before taking action. Indeed, she is at times indecisive and does make mistakes. Eventually, however, the officers come to respect her. As in *The Gentle Touch*, plots deal with social issues and with the protagonist's personal life. Inspector Darblay is married, and her husband is at first unemployed and later trapped and underemployed due to his wife's promotion in a region of England with few jobs.

In later episodes, Inspector Darblay is promoted to another posting, and Inspector Kate Longton (Anna Cartaret) is assigned to head the Hartley section. Inspector Longton's status as a single woman presented a variety of plot options. Sydney-Smith (2009, 51) reports that Cartaret suggested to the program's producers that her character might possibly be a lesbian. Her suggestion was rejected. Instead, Inspector Longton has some romantic involvements, including a relationship with another police officer (Sydney-Smith 2009, 52).

Cagney & Lacey (1981–88) was a groundbreaking US police procedural that entered the television schedule during this same era. Tyne Daly starred as Mary Beth Lacey, a working-class woman who was married and the mother of two sons. Sharon Gless played Christine Cagney. Cagney was single and dated men but had no interest in marriage; she also came from a higher social class than did Lacey. Set in New York City, plots dealt with crimes, but the series also addressed social issues, especially issues that were important to women such as abortion, breast cancer, sexual harassment, and battered women (e.g., in one story, the abusive man was a police officer). Barbara Avedon and Barbara Corday, who developed *Cagney & Lacey* and wrote many of the scripts, created a series that was aimed at a female audience. Julie D'Acci (1994), in her excellent and detailed analysis of *Cagney & Lacey*, recounts the interesting origin of the series. Avedon and Corday had read Molly Haskell's treatise *From Reverence to Rape: The Treatment of Women in the Movies* and were frustrated that neither film nor television had featured a women's buddy format of the sort that was commonplace among men. They developed a series that featured two women police officers who were partners and friends. The two writers gave the script to Barney Rosenszwig, who would produce the series. For a time, he had produced *Charlie's Angels*. They also gave Rosenszwig a copy of Haskell's classic treatise (Mizejewski 2004, 69).

D'Acci (1994) and other feminist scholars (e.g., Gledhill 1988) note that *Cagney & Lacey* generated many challenges for television programming. First, the program challenged the male-oriented traditions of the police procedural. D'Acci (1994) notes that these issues were a problem for producers even before the series began. Initially, network executives conditioned approval for the series on securing sexy movie stars like Ann-Margret and Raquel Welch to play Cagney and Lacey. These actresses were unavailable, and the pilot starred Tyne Daly as Lacey and Loretta Swit as Cagney. Swit was unavailable for the series, so the producers chose Meg Foster to play Cagney, but the network executives vetoed Foster because she had played a lesbian in a made-for-television movie, and this created a "problematic lesbian connection" for a series about two women (D'Acci 1994). Even when the executives accepted Sharon Gless in the role, Cagney's marital status concerned them; press writers saw her as not sufficiently feminine. The focus on social issues, especially those that were aimed at women, was viewed by some executives as too political, too "women's lib." D'Acci (1994) details the constant pressure from television executives to address these concerns. Despite good ratings and critical acclaim (the series, Daly, and Gless all won Emmys), the network canceled *Cagney & Lacey*. The National Organization for Women (NOW) mounted a letter-writing campaign that for a time saved the series (D'Acci 1994).

Sydney-Smith (2009) suggests that *Cagney & Lacey* sometimes became overly melodramatic, especially for a police procedural. Even so, most scholars agree that the series was a landmark in US programming, especially in the police procedural, because of its portrayal of two women as professionals, partners, and friends. The program revealed the obvious nuances of difference among women (e.g., marital status, social class, even styles of policing). Moreover, the focus on social issues continued an important shift in the crime genre that had already begun in the UK.

The Gentle Touch, *Juliet Bravo*, and *Cagney & Lacey* were pivotal for the television police procedural in the UK and the United States. They featured women in lead roles, which was significant for television generally but particularly for the traditionally male-oriented police procedural. Equally important, television circulates images about what is and what is not possible in social life, and these programs presented the idea that women could succeed in a male-identified profession. The protagonists confronted sexism in their professional lives (as did real policewomen), and their personal lives were touched by a variety of issues that were relevant to women, including, for example, issues of work/life balance that confront all workers but especially women who work in demanding occupations. To varying degrees, these series continued the trend toward realism in the procedural but, significantly, with women as protagonists. In short, these programs challenged the genre conventions that had been so unfriendly to women.

These 1980s women-centered police procedurals were the backdrop for the *Prime Suspect* series. Beginning with the first episode in 1991, *Prime Suspect* took up where its predecessors left off. The sexism that Jane Tennison confronts is more interpersonally vitriolic than that experienced by her fictional predecessors; moreover, it is steeped in and protected by organizational patriarchy. The series exhibited *The Sweeney*'s hectic pace while maintaining and expanding the depiction of police routines that were the basis of *Hill Street Blues*, routines that are the defining element of the police procedural. *Prime Suspect* thus built on the tradition of male-centric procedurals even as it followed in the path of *The Gentle Touch*, *Juliet Bravo*, and *Cagney & Lacey*. Indeed, years later, in her acceptance speech for a US Emmy, Helen Mirren acknowledged *Cagney & Lacey* for opening the way for a series like *Prime Suspect* (Walton and Jones 1999, 289).

It is not surprising that *Prime Suspect*, given its success and in-your-face challenge to more traditional police procedurals, has been the focus of much scholarly analysis. Some of these analyses are critical of the series and Tennison character. Media scholars such as Abercrombie (1996), Nunn and Biressi (2003), Thornham (1994), and Tomc (1995) argue that, notwithstanding *Prime Suspect*'s obvious place in the pantheon of television police drama, it is ultimately trapped by the genre's standard conventions as well as by the strictures of television: the series privileges social control (police catching criminals), not institutional change. In her treatise on women detectives, Mizejewski (2004) argues that Jane Tennison is no renegade; instead, she is a careerist who strives to advance in the police hierarchy. Thornham (1994) suggests that to the degree that *Prime Suspect* contains any feminist inflection, it is of the liberal, equal opportunity variety. Media scholar Deborah Jermyn (2010) suggests that *Prime Suspect* is a police drama, not a progressive women's police drama. Jermyn and other scholars (e.g., Brooks 1994) point out that although Tennison is often badly treated by the police hierarchy, she herself mistreats women subordinates: she questions their competence and their loyalty. Indeed, Tennison seems unconnected to other women, either professionally or personally. Glenn Creeber (2001) suggests that Tennison's careerism isolates her to the point that she seems to be a casualty of feminism; that is, her pursuit of a career comes at the cost of any personal life.

Some critics and scholars (e.g., Press 1991; Eaton 1995) utilize the term "postfeminist" to describe programs that imply feminism has resulted in women's employment and consequent loss of love and family connections. Along these lines, they categorize *Prime Suspect* as a postfeminist program. The label postfeminism has also been applied to programs that convey a sense that feminism is simply no longer needed because women have achieved equality; clearly, *Prime Suspect* conveys almost the opposite message. In any event, we disagree with blanket negative characterizations of *Prime Suspect* as postfeminist and see the series as more nuanced than such critiques imply.

We argue in this book that, notwithstanding its limitations, *Prime Suspect* significantly alters the police procedural drama through its realistic portrait of women's struggles to integrate into police occupations. Drawing on the model of progressive moral fiction that we develop in Chapter 1 (also see Cavender and Jurik 2004), we will identify insights into the contextual roots of crime and limitations of the police and legal system that are offered in the *Prime Suspect* series. We describe instances in which the Tennison character serves as a provocateur for justice. Finally, we suggest that the use of our model and this series provides an effective pedagogical device for teaching about gender and justice issues.

The Chapters to Follow

In the following six chapters, we elaborate our model and analysis of *Prime Suspect*, including the tension between Jane Tennison as justice provocateur and Jane Tennison as postfeminist icon. In Chapter 1, "Analytic Framework," we discuss the history and key elements of a feminist crime genre that has emerged over the past thirty years. While this genre flourished more in novels than in film or television, we elaborate how police procedurals, arguably including *Prime Suspect*, are now more common in television and in a subgenre that has been especially resistant to women in lead roles. We draw on the elements of a feminist crime genre to develop our model for a progressive moral fiction. We discuss the intellectual predecessors and defining elements of this approach. We will then use our model to examine specific episodes and the entire oeuvre of *Prime Suspect*, including its consistencies and inconsistencies with our ideal of progressive moral fiction. A brief overview of the seven *Prime Suspect* episodes in the series is provided in the Appendix.

Prime Suspect offers one of the most in-depth looks at the resistance to women in policing during the first couple of decades of women's more complete integration into the field. In Chapter 2, "*Prime Suspect* and Women in Policing," we examine how the portrayal of women police officers in the *Prime Suspect* series comports with the lived experiences of actual policewomen, in particular, those who occupy higher ranks within police organizations. We draw on the large body of research findings that have documented women's experiences in policing, and we highlight the insights of four veteran women officers and police administrators working in the London Metropolitan Police.

Chapter 3, "Investigating and Challenging," examines Tennison's strategies for overcoming gender barriers and solving cases. Tennison challenges organizational and interpersonal barriers to successfully perform her job. In doing her job, she demonstrates a relentless work ethic, attention to the details of the case, aggressiveness, trickery, and at times what might seem to be special "feminine" insights. We also argue that Tennison's sense of justice for victims motivates her investigations.

In Chapter 4, "Doing Justice," we examine elements of a feminist and progressive moral fiction that we observe in the *Prime Suspect* series. The crime genre has traditionally presented a variety of ideologies, from critiques of dominant institutions to a more conservative law-and-order ideology. Increasingly over the past twenty-five years, US television crime drama has offered a more conservative ideological stance. In contrast, we suggest that the *Prime Suspect* series conveys a more complicated sense of justice. Tennison operates within the law but understands its limitations. This understanding, however, motivates action, not cynicism, and Tennison often acts as a provocateur for justice. We also discuss the ways in which conflicts in the viewpoints and actions of various characters and inconsistencies in Tennison's own actions actually encourage debate about the most just solutions in each case.

In Chapter 5, "Private Troubles and Public Issues," we discuss *Prime Suspect*'s treatment of social problems and socially marginalized individuals. The series resembles a 1940s type of film, the social problems film, but with a focus on contemporary issues. It conveys a sense of the plight of socially marginalized groups in ways that identify some of the societal-level roots of these problems. Topics include sexism and racism in policing, child sexual abuse, and immigration. We discuss narrative and aesthetic devices (e.g., camera work, scene composition) that work to position Tennison with the victims of crimes. The often invisible life and work experiences as well as the humanity of socially marginalized victims are made visible in the series.

In Chapter 6, "*Prime Suspect* and Progressive Moral Fiction," we discuss the strengths and limitations of *Prime Suspect* as a work of progressive moral fiction. We identify ways that the conventions of the crime genre and the strictures of television work against the transformative potential of the series. We elaborate apparent flaws in the character of Jane Tennison: incidents of personality issues and unethical behavior that appear in the series. Again drawing on literature and original data, we discuss how her shortcomings reflect issues faced by real-life policewomen as well as issues of work/life balance more generally. We suggest that Tennison's flaws can actually enhance debates about gender and justice. In this chapter, we draw on the work of feminist critical race scholar Patricia Hill Collins (2000) in her work *Black Feminist Thought* to describe a "both/and" perspective for understanding Tennison's character. She is both a provocateur for justice and a flawed human being. We compare *Prime Suspect* with several other contemporary police procedural dramas. At the end of this chapter, we briefly describe the theoretical and pedagogical implications of *Prime Suspect* and our model of progressive moral fiction. We will focus on how our model can be used in the classroom to address the justice implications in *Prime Suspect* and media productions more generally.

CHAPTER 1

Analytic Framework

In this chapter, we develop our framework for analyzing *Prime Suspect*. It is our intention that this framework serve as a benchmark for examining gender and justice issues in cultural productions, including film and television. In contrast to some cultural studies approaches that claim to avoid value assessments of fictional works, we adopt an approach that not only examines but advocates for works that promote hopes for and actions toward social justice.

The first component of our framework rests on the idea that a feminist crime genre has emerged in the past few decades. As noted in the Introduction, the crime genre has historically either excluded women or presented them in subordinate and stereotypical roles. After this long, male-dominated history, the crime genre increasingly features women as producers of and protagonists in the genre. This change has altered the genre by decentering the domination of male protagonists and their methods for understanding and solving crimes. Scholars have identified other significant features of the emerging feminist crime genre: it looks beyond individuals to attend to structural roots of crime and related social problems; there tends to be less violence in such works; the protagonist demonstrates an ethic of responsibility toward victims in promoting just solutions to the case.

We drew inspiration from these discussions of a feminist crime genre to develop a second and interrelated component of our framework of analysis, a model of what we call progressive moral fiction. Some scholars have called for an increasing identification and production of factual and fictional/dramatic works that inspire others to do justice and transform unjust social arrangements. With regard to the crime genre, works of progressive moral fiction may include story lines that reveal the social systemic nature and context of criminal actions and that feature socially marginalized victims and a protagonist who understands the limitations of law and is dedicated to helping victims. We also draw on the work of other literary, feminist, and critical race theorists to formulate our ideal type model of progressive moral fiction. We will argue that our model can be used as a framework for media research and for using media to teach about gender and justice issues.

The Feminist Crime Genre

Despite a number of successful women contributors, the crime genre has been largely a male preserve. In her treatise on women detectives, Maureen Reddy (1988, 5) argues that the crime genre was characterized by disruption (the crime), linear progress toward order, the banishment of disruptive elements, and ultimately the preservation by a male authority of the bourgeois order and patriarchy. Reddy and other experts on women's crime fiction (e.g., Munt 1994; Klein 1995) viewed the crime genre as a primarily conservative and masculine form that reinforced masculine dominance.

The first fictional British woman police detective appeared in 1864 in a book called *The Female Detective*. The book was "edited" by Andrew Forrester, although Kathleen Klein (1995, 18) suggests that this was a fictional work, not a police casebook. The author variously referred to the protagonist as Miss or Mrs. Gladden and denied the audience details about her life as a woman so as to focus more on her portrayal as a detective (Klein 1995, 18). A second volume featuring a woman police detective quickly followed: W. Stephens Hayward's *The Experiences of a Lady Detective*. The protagonist, a Mrs. Paschal, was a widow who joined the police force because she was lacking in income (Klein 1995, 24). These two volumes generated no immediate imitators in a woman's subgenre. Women detectives appeared later in the nineteenth century in the United States as a part of the dime novel tradition. However, Klein (1995, 24) notes that there were very few woman-centered stories and that the men writers who featured women as protagonists tended to undercut them by foregrounding romance and marriage as events that would end the woman's role as an investigator.

Thus, women appeared in the crime genre but did not alter the view that detection was a masculine pursuit (Munt 1994). There were no (or few) women investigators in the real world, so there was no believable environment for them in the crime genre (Klein 1992).

Discussions of a women's crime genre begin with consideration of "mystery" crime novels. Famous early women mystery novelists included Agatha Christie and Dorothy Sayers. Agatha Christie (1890–1976) is one of the best-selling authors of all time, and her mystery series heroes included Miss Jane Marple, small English village wise woman, and Hercule Poirot, eccentric Belgian male detective. Dorothy Sayers's (1893–1957) books featured an aristocratic amateur sleuth, Lord Peter Wimsey, who solved numerous mysteries and was especially popular in the 1930s and 1940s. Wimsey had a romantic interest in the novels, Harriet Vane, who is a mystery writer and sometimes also an amateur sleuth. She rejects Wimsey's many marriage proposals in Sayers's earlier novels, but they marry in *Busman's Honeymoon* (1937). Christie, Sayers, and other women writers in what was initially a British literary tradition (e.g., Josephine Tey, Ngaio Marsh) were labeled as part of a "cozy" subgenre. A cozy is a mystery that contains little violence, sex, or tough language. Typically, the main character is a good, likeable woman or man who is an amateur detective and identifies the criminal through an intuitive or intellectual examination of the crime scene, suspects, and clues. At the end of the story, the criminal is apprehended, and order is restored. Cozies were usually set among the elite, often in a sedate countryside setting or vacation atmosphere, and were associated with women authors and women audiences (Walton and Jones 1999).

The hard-boiled crime novel is a different literary style that most often is associated with the urban United States and with professional detectives (and later with police) who are tough and sometimes flawed heroes. These novels include considerably more violence and sex than the novels of the cozy tradition. The beginning of this style is associated with US writers such as Carroll John Daly in the mid-1920s, but its huge increase in popularity is most often attributed to the work of Dashiell Hammett and Raymond Chandler in the 1930s and 1940s. Their stories initially appeared in pulp magazines. Even though they were later published as novels, these books are still referred to as pulp fiction. Hard-boiled detectives were almost always men. Hard-boiled authors and fans disparaged cozies as too soft and feminized (Walton and Jones 1999). Moreover, in an oft-quoted essay, Raymond Chandler offered harsh criticism of Agatha Christie and the cozy tradition for their class and cultural elitism and lack of realism (Walton and Jones 1999). He claimed that the hard-boiled tradition led by Hammett "gave murder back to the kind of people that commit it for reasons, not just to provide a corpse. . . . He put these people down on paper as they were, and he made them talk and think in the language they customarily used" (Chandler 1946, 222). Hard-boiled detective novels were more likely to include women characters but portray them in negative ways that we will discuss later.

Like the hard-boiled subgenre, the police procedural subgenre pioneered by another US author, Hillary Waugh (a man) (1920–2008), sought urban realism, this time through careful portrayals of routine police work. Early procedural novels largely excluded women as key characters or portrayed women in subordinated and stereotyped roles (if at all) (Hirsch 1981). Table 1.1 provides examples of each of the three crime subgenres.

Feminists have long been critical of the crime genre's depiction of women, who, when not entirely ignored, were often relegated to the roles of victims, lovers, and temptresses. They describe how cozies, which feature

Table 1.1. Examples of Subgenre Types

Subgenre Types	Novels	Films or Television Series
Cozies	Agatha Christie's Miss Marple series Agatha Christie's Poirot series Dorothy Sayers's Lord Peter Wimsey series	*Murder, She Wrote* *Midsomer Murders* *Nancy Drew* *The Hardy Boys* *Hetty Wainthropp*
Hard-boiled	Dashiell Hammett's Sam Spade Dorothy Hughes's Dix Steele Raymond Chandler's Philip Marlowe Margaret Millar's Tom Aragon	*Peter Gunn* *Mannix* *Chinatown* *Veronica Mars*
Police procedural	Ed McBain's 57th Precinct series John Creasey's West Scotland Yard series Joseph Wambaugh's novels about the LAPD Lynda La Plante's police novels Elizabeth George's Inspector Lynley series	*Dragnet* *Hill Street Blues* *The Bill* *The Sweeney* *The Gentle Touch* *Juliet Bravo* *Cagney & Lacey* *NYPD Blue*

women as chief protagonists, were demeaned as unrealistic or as less serious "mysteries" as opposed to more male-centered, hard-boiled, "crime" genre works. Historically, much of the hard-boiled crime genre has been so misogynistic that Klein (1995), in a play on the title of a P. D. James novel (later a British television crime series), lamented that the role of the professional detective was "an unsuitable job for a woman."

Despite its male-dominated history, a few women writers (e.g., Dorothy B. Hughes and Vera Caspary) did gain some success in the hard-boiled tradition during the 1930s and 1940s. Their now-classic novels, Hughes's *In a Lonely Place* (1947) and Caspary's *Laura* (1943), also became successful films. These writers influenced other hard-boiled and suspense novelists, several of whom were also women. For example, Elizabeth Sanxay Holding (1889–1955) was described by Raymond Chandler as one of the top writers of detective and suspense fiction. Margaret Millar (1915–94), who has been recognized for her intelligent portrayals of women's psyches, dealt with issues of sexual freedom, madness, and hypocritical moral codes that were shaped by class position. One of her protagonists was a Latino lawyer named Tom Aragon. In contrast to much other hard-boiled fiction, these novelists featured women in strong roles, although not as police officers or professional detectives. When their novels featured investigators, these roles were generally occupied by men.

The number of crime novels written by women began to sharply increase in the late 1970s, and the upward slope of that increase became even more pronounced in the 1980s and 1990s (Klein 1992; Walton and Jones 1999). Although not all of these novels featured women investigators, the number of crime novels with women protagonists exploded in the mid-1980s and has tripled every five years since 1985 (Mizejewski 2004, 19). A by-product of the growth in women's crime fiction has been the appearance of numerous scholarly treatises on women's crime fiction (see Reddy 1988; Munt 1994; Klein 1995; Walton and Jones 1999).

Dorie Klein (1992) and others (e.g., Klein 1995; Reddy 1988, 2003; Walton and Jones 1999; Mizejewski 2004) who analyze women's crime fiction agree that such works exhibit features that distinguish them from the traditional male-centered crime genre. These works offer images of strong and independent investigators in a variety of settings such as private detectives, police homicide detectives, FBI agents, and forensic pathologists. These novels also deal with women's experiences of workplace discrimination and victimization (Walton and Jones 1999). Plots tend to feature crimes that are linked to social problems or to the larger social structure; indeed, Klein (1995) notes that, unlike more traditional male-centered works, social disruption, not crime, often drives these stories. Unlike much of the traditional crime genre, women detectives are not appendages to men; they may be single, have a support group of other women, or be involved in lesbian relationships (e.g., Katherine Forrest's Kate Delafield novels and Laurie King's Kate Martinelli series). Several sources (e.g., Klein 1992; Klein 1995) suggest that there is less violence in the feminist crime genre and that if violence occurs, it is less glorified and less sensationalized, and the depictions convey the negative outcomes of violent acts. Klein (1995) and Mizejewski (2004) conclude that where men detectives answer to an internal moral code, women detectives, in line with arguments of scholars such as Carol Gilligan (1982), are driven by an ethic of social responsibility and compassion toward victims. Feminist crime fiction confronts issues of sexual orientation, class bias, corporate corruption, and racism.

Barbara Neely has developed a series of crime novels focused on amateur detective Blanche White, who is an African American woman working as a maid (the novels are set in New England and the southern United States). Because she is a domestic worker and a woman of color, Blanche and her domestic worker colleagues are often treated as invisible by other white and more elite members of society, including police and professional detectives. As a result of this marginalized status and her keen observational and deductive skills, Blanche is able to see, hear, and know things that go unheard or unobserved by others. The novels present captivating mysteries that simultaneously result in a solution to the crime but also a better understanding of racism and the limits of law in a racist society.

Women appeared as police officers in television crime dramas about the same time that women entered police patrol work in greater numbers. They were cast in ensembles and in a few starring roles (e.g., *Police Woman* in the 1970s and *The Gentle Touch* in the 1980s). Given women's real-world occupational changes, institutionalized sexism was an available plot device in these police programs (Mizejewski 2004). This shift in procedurals occurred amidst a trend toward women-centered programming in television more generally (Walton and Jones 1999; Mizejewski 2004). By the 2000s, the television crime genre increasingly featured strong, independent women investigators in a variety of settings such as street cops and police homicide detectives.

The relatively greater presence of women in television programming when compared to that of film is related to both the proportionate size of women television audiences and the lower costs of television productions. These factors converge to make television producers more willing to experiment with women characters and women's issues (Rapping 1992; Mizejewski 2004).

Even procedurals that feature women protagonists are often trapped by male-centered conventions. These productions typically adopt a liberal, equal opportunity kind of feminism and do not intend to fundamentally alter the genre. Nevertheless, several scholars argue that casting women in central roles goes well beyond producer intent and control (Walton and Jones 1999; Johnston 1999). Women detectives are not merely substitutes for men; their presence literally changes the genre and produces critiques of such important dimensions of the formula as the nature of authority, which no longer remains a male preserve, and the form of justice provided by the criminal justice system. These productions give women a greater sense of agency and resistance and promote a deeper sense of justice than law alone provides. Genres change with the times (Mittell 2004), but some argue that feminism changed the crime genre to such an extent that it comprises an entirely new form (Reddy 1988; Klein 1995; Sydney-Smith 2009). Dorie Klein (1992) utilizes the label—a feminist crime genre—to refer to novels, but we expand the usage of her term to include women-centered television and film productions.

Most feminist critiques of the crime genre focus their attention on women's infiltration and deconstruction of more hard-boiled works and thereby understate the accomplishments and continued importance of women-centered elements within the cozy tradition. These critiques also tend to overlook the possibility for blending the so-called feminine cozy with masculinist hard-boiled traditions. For example, Lidia Curti (1988) discusses blends of feminine-associated soap opera plots and narrative styles with more masculine police procedural–style narratives in 1980s police dramas such as *Hill Street Blues*, *Juliet Bravo*, *The Gentle Touch*, and *Cagney & Lacey*. As noted in the Introduction, these procedurals combined the police procedural genre with subplots about the personal lives and

conflicts of series characters. Curti (1988) also notes that they combine
a linear with a circular narrative style. These programs combine some of
the eccentric characters and humor that were historically part of the cozy
tradition with more hard-boiled elements of adventure and suspense.

In addition, discussions of an emerging feminist genre (e.g., Klein 1992;
Walton and Jones 1999; Mizejewski 2004) often undervalue women's earlier, limited entries into the hard-boiled subgenre. As evidenced from our
discussion of the 1930s and 1940s, hard-boiled women crime writers, intelligent portraits of women, and a sensitivity to issues of class, war, and
other societal problems originated before the women-centered writers of
the 1970s and 1980s. Nevertheless, the growth in numbers and popularity
of such works does mark recent decades as a watershed for more feminist inspired crime fiction. However, the pioneering women's hard-boiled
writings of the 1930s and 1940s continue to influence the crime genre. For
example, Hughes's book *In a Lonely Place* is often cited as an influence
on Patricia Highsmith's novel and film *The Talented Mr. Ripley*. Holding's
novel *The Blank Wall* was made into a movie in 1949 and remade in 2001
as *The Deep End* starring Tilda Swinton.

Thus, crime genre productions authored by and featuring women have
existed for almost 150 years. Beginning in the 1970s, these stories escalated
in popularity and so altered the genre as to arguably constitute a feminist
crime genre. There is an audience for this work because it includes stories
that are informed by feminism and that are relevant to women. Moreover, a
defining element of the feminist crime genre is its focus on social justice. In
the next section, we merge elements of the feminist crime genre with other
writings about fiction and social justice pursuits to develop our model of
progressive moral fiction. We now turn to a discussion of this model.

Progressive Moral Fiction and Justice Provocateurs

In previous analyses of *Prime Suspect* and other television programs (see
Cavender and Jurik 2004, 2007, 2010; Adelman, Cavender, and Jurik 2009),
we have developed an ideal type model for assessing the progressive potential of cultural productions, in particular with regard to issues of gender, race, sexuality, and social justice. Our model draws on tenets of the
feminist crime genre.

Of course, some cultural studies scholars deem it to be inappropriate to provide value assessments of cultural products, focusing instead on how these products signify meanings and how they are consumed (Butler 2007). Other scholars disagree with this position. Jason Mittell (2009) argues that scholars frequently engage in value assessments albeit through disguised language, noting, for example, that a cultural production is complex or compelling. Instead of this backdoor approach, Mittell (2009, 123) advocates for assessments that are premised on defensible elements of evaluation. He sees these assessments not as an "incontrovertible fact" that ends discussions but rather as a judgment that opens a dialogue about a cultural production. Similarly, British cultural historian Raymond Williams (1989) urges scholars and critics to make note of and applaud good cultural productions in the hope of encouraging more good works. Novelist and literary critic John Gardner (1982) praised what he termed "moral fiction." For Gardner, fiction is moral when it "presents valid models for imitation" and when it offers a "vision of the possible which can inspire and incite human beings toward virtue" (1982, 18). Feminist critical race theorist Angela Davis (1999) argues that art can indeed inspire individuals to work for social transformation.

Consistent with these scholars, we seek out and analyze cultural productions in the crime genre that not only provide the occasional, necessary respite from discouraging and oppressive societal conditions (e.g., Griffith 2005) but also, more importantly, expand concerns about and encourage actions that promote social and economic equality and democratic participation. In addition to drawing insights from media and cultural studies, we were also inspired in our quest to develop a model of progressive moral fiction by a variety of works from outside the media-cultural studies area, including writings by feminist critical race theorists and legal scholars (e.g., Romero 2001; Smith 1979; Collins 2000).

Our model of progressive moral fiction is informed by scholarship about just societies, especially by the work of feminist political theorist Iris Marion Young. Young addressed the possibility of such societies in philosophically informed public policy scholarship. In one case, for example, Young (1994) discussed self-proclaimed empowerment rehabilitation programs. She suggested that any program aiming to empower participants should include dialogues about their life experiences and trace the social organizational arrangements that give rise to their problems as individuals. Young's approach is consistent with that of feminist sociologist Dorothy Smith (1979), who called for an analysis of the everyday experiences of socially marginalized individuals and an examination of the social organizational processes that give rise to their problems. Young (1994) concluded her analysis of empowerment programs with an outline for a more progressive model in such endeavors, including the suggestion that such programs should facilitate connections among participants and other organizations in ways that might promote collective action for social change.

Young's comments are a part of a larger project wherein she considers patterns of injustice and social policies that would produce a just society. She details these views in *Justice and the Politics of Difference* (1990). Injustice for Young has two dimensions: domination results when people are structurally excluded from self-determination; oppression results from the inability to express and fulfill human capabilities (1990, 40, 32). Justice entails social arrangements that encourage people to develop and exercise their capabilities and to have a voice in determining their lives. Young (1990) articulates a progressive vision of the just and fair society that embraces rather than denies difference: she argues that people must have a voice in societal decision making both at work and in government as well as the opportunity for social recognition and self-fulfillment.

Other scholars offer compatible views. In his statement of progressive moral values, George Lakoff (2006) includes empathy as the capacity to connect and feel kinship with other people and responsibility for oneself and others. Lakoff stresses the importance of making clear statements and analyses of fundamental progressive values. Elizabeth Segal (2007) also articulates a concept that she calls "social empathy" as a part of public policy. Social empathy entails a commitment to understand the lived experiences of those who are socially marginalized and then taking social responsibility, that is, creating policies or even taking personal actions to improve those lives. For Segal (2007), social empathy is an impetus to produce social justice.

These ideas of Lakoff, Segal, and Young figured prominently in our formulation of a model of progressive moral fiction. We wanted to go beyond political theory or public policy and to instead reconfigure these ideas as a way to evaluate works of fiction for their potential to inspire social justice. These analyses of social empathy, progressive values, and a commitment to a just society suggest elements that we think are appropriate in our model.

Accordingly, we identify four elements of a progressive moral fiction to include the following:

- Insights from the experiences of the socially marginalized and oppressed
- A locating of these experiences within some larger social context
- Revelations of fissures in the predominant ruling apparatus
- Glimpses of hope for individual and/or collective efforts to challenge unjust social arrangements

In attempting to identify and analyze works of progressive moral fiction, we also draw on Jane Aiken's (2001) concept of justice provocateur, a label that describes her approach to law school pedagogy. According to Aiken (1997), the mission of law professors, and especially clinicians, is to teach future lawyers how to promote justice in their law practices. She trains students to work with the law but also to understand its limitations. They learn that neither the law nor the state is a neutral agent and that justice does not somehow reside in the technical or neutral application of rules. They also learn to identify inequality and injustices perpetuated by the law. There are few absolute answers, and law students must be sensitive to complexity, contradiction, and nuance and learn the "skill of compassion." Aiken urges students to move beyond legal relativism, cynicism, and powerlessness in order to find ways to use law to promote justice and, when possible, to work for social transformation. She focuses on law students in legal clinics because they can learn to hear the voices of their clients, who typically are socially marginalized people. Her pedagogy aims to inspire students to feel empowered to promote positive change. We believe that Aiken's concept can also be applied to an analysis of crime genre protagonists (Cavender and Jurik 2004, 2007). We ask in what way they are consistent with and/or contradict Aiken's model of justice provocateurs.

A progressive moral fiction and the justice provocateur imagery challenge many of the verities of criminology and contemporary media discourse. Crime and justice are not understood within the narrow strictures of law and criminal justice but instead are understood as residing within larger social structures. With regard to the crime genre, this analytic frame avoids a simplistic law-and-order perspective of bad guys versus good guys and a world-weary cynicism in which all is relative. A progressive moral fiction offers hope for individuals to contribute to positive social change. Of course, we are mindful that cultural productions seldom offer uniformly progressive or reactionary images of either gender or justice. We do not argue that every aspect or scene in a work or indeed that every work must be consistent with our progressive moral fiction model. This model is rather intended to be used as a benchmark device to provoke discussion and analysis. It is a means of searching out and identifying the possible presence and absence of progressive and moral dimensions in a single work or for making comparisons across cultural productions. Next, we provide a description of our methodological approach for analyzing *Prime Suspect*.

Our Methodological Approach to the Analysis

We utilize an interpretative approach in our analysis of *Prime Suspect*. Although we are social scientists with traditional methodological training, we do not offer an analysis that is based on a random selection of scenes or that is validated by claims of intercoder reliability. Rather than hypothesis testing, we present scenes and dialogue from the episodes as heuristic devices that exemplify both the progressive and the feminist potential as well as the conservative tendencies of the crime genre. We are also sensitive to the fact that the plots and scenes that we describe could generate alternate readings other than those we offer; we discuss these alternate readings as they have appeared in the scholarly and popular literature.

Although we will present evidence from key interviews (e.g., actors, producers, writers, and directors) about the *Prime Suspect* series, we do not claim that the scenes we describe are in all cases an intentional outcome. Cultural productions are the product of social interactions located within particular social historical contexts; they rely on specific media technologies and conventions (Smith 1999). Cultural productions take on a reality of their own, just as do real-life interactions, and that reality is always emergent and may change with subsequent viewings over time. Thus, we analyze *Prime Suspect* as a social-cultural production and are especially interested in its implications for challenging the crime genre and television's traditions. Regardless of the actual conscious or unconscious intent, we examine the ways in which the series challenges and reinforces the traditional male-gaze stance common to the police procedural subgenre.

Given the interpretative nature of our study, we should locate ourselves as researchers. We are fans of the crime genre; however, as feminists and progressives, we are uncomfortable with its traditionally racist and misogynistic content. As fans and as scholars, we are drawn to the feminist crime genre. Based upon in-depth analysis of the *Prime Suspect* series and our viewing of a wide array of other crime drama (Cavender and Jurik 2010), we began to develop a model of progressive moral fiction as a tool to analyze fictional works including and beyond *Prime Suspect*. This model was developed for our research and for teaching our students to critically assess media productions.

As noted, we do not argue that every scene in the series does or should exemplify progressive and feminist principles in action. In addition to specific plots and scenes that are consistent with our model of progressive moral fiction, we also present examples that illustrate the conservative tendencies of traditional police procedurals, those that limit notions of justice and negatively stereotype women. Our analysis also identifies areas of nuance, complexity, and contradiction that reflect issues confronting women in contemporary society and would-be justice provocateurs. It is these inconsistencies that will stimulate critical discussions about social justice.

Conclusion

In summary, our model directs attention to how much a cultural product portrays the structural context of individual problems, that is, to what extent it connects personal troubles with public issues. In the case of the crime genre in particular, do series narratives and dialogue locate crime within a societal context? To what degree is the series embedded within a feminist crime genre? To what degree and in what ways are the characters provocateurs for justice? Do they or the series as a whole challenge or reinforce traditionally taken-for-granted notions of legal and criminal justice? Does the cultural work provide a sense of space in which individuals and/or social groups might act as justice provocateurs to promote social justice?

We wish to encourage individual and social discussion, debate, and action. We recognize that progressive works may entail contradictory moments with characters who are flawed and whose actions or experiences may at times reinforce status quo social arrangements. Here we borrow from feminist critical race scholar Patricia Hill Collins (2000), who argues that social scientists (and, we would add, media scholars) must move beyond either/or assessments to understand that social life is complex and that real phenomena and cultural products can both be transformational and reproduce existing strictures. Good fiction/drama should reflect some of the contradiction and the complexity of the real world. We look at the degree to which this work ultimately offers glimpses of the need for change and the potential for increased social justice. We believe that the *Prime Suspect* series offers an opportunity to examine these contradictions through both the presentation of Tennison's character and the competing definitions of crime and justice conveyed in the series. In the next chapter, we take up Tennison's experiences as a woman police investigator and compare these to the lived experiences of real policewomen. In later chapters, we consider Tennison's methods of investigation, sense of justice, and contextualization of the crimes she investigates to consider to what degree she constitutes a justice provocateur and to what extent the series challenges taken-for-granted conceptions of law and social justice.

CHAPTER 2

Prime Suspect and Women in Policing

To a large extent, the early absence of women police protagonists from novels and television programs was an accurate reflection of social reality. As we discussed in the Introduction, women were largely excluded from the majority of police patrol and crime investigation jobs until the 1970s. Despite their integration into a wider range of police duties, women continued to struggle to remain and advance in their positions and often were relegated to police work that was behind the scenes of street patrol and investigation. Such jobs were hardly the "stuff" of crime fiction. We begin this chapter with a discussion of the experiences of real-world women working in policing after the 1970s integration period. Then we elaborate the ways in which *Prime Suspect 1* brought the feminist genre to the television police procedural form, a subgenre that has been especially resistant to women in lead roles. In the final section of this chapter, we reflect on how the portrayal of women police officers in the *Prime Suspect* series comports with the lived experiences of actual policewomen, in particular, those who occupy high ranks in police organizations.

Real-World Experiences of Women in Policing after 1970s Integration

When police departments began to assign women to a full range of police duties, an overt, extensive, and continuing opposition to policewomen occurred at all levels in the UK, the United States, and numerous other countries (Brown and Heidensohn 2000; Martin and Jurik 2007). This resistance often flew in the face of official departmental policies of equal opportunity. The integration policies also effectively ended specialized women's divisions begun in the early twentieth century. Ironically, the disestablishment of special women's divisions dramatically reduced the numbers and percentages of women who occupied highly ranked police positions in the years immediately following integration (Brown 1998).

Research has documented both the advancements of and barriers faced by women police officers in the 1980s through the 1990s (Martin 1980; Morash and Greene 1986; Hunt 1990; Brown and Fielding 1993; Brown 1998; Brown and Heidensohn 2000; Jurik and Martin 2001). Women's duties and numbers have slowly expanded in UK and US police departments since the 1970s, and women now comprise about 15 percent of sworn police personnel (Brown and Heidensohn 2000; Martin and Jurik 2007). Police-women have faced barriers to parity with policemen at the interpersonal, organizational, and societal levels.

As numerical tokens (15 percent or less), women officers' visibility was heightened (Kanter 1977; Brown and Heidensohn 2000). This visibility, combined with negative expectations about women's policing abilities, subjected them to greater scrutiny than men. To be viewed as minimally competent, women had to exceed normal work expectations. Yet highly competent women threatened male coworkers and the solidarity of the all-male work group. As outsiders, women undermined the historical links between good police work and masculine prowess (Smith and Gray 1985; Brown 2007). To the extent that police work and masculine identity were intertwined, women's success in policing was a challenge to policemen's sense of self (Martin 1980). Moreover, visions of women as symbolic keepers of moral virtue threatened policemen who participated in or knew of corrupt police practices (Hunt 1990).

Initially, policewomen were isolated through a variety of behaviors, including inattention, ridicule, and outright hostility. Male citizens often demonstrated resistance to women officers through subtle nonverbal cues as well as verbal insults and, less frequently, physical assaults (Martin 1980). Policemen stereotyped women officers as either little sister/dependent types, motherly types, promiscuous whore types, or stern iron maiden types (Martin 1980). A unifying feature of much of policemen's resistance was the sexualization of women in the workplace. Women's sexual orientation and marital status were the subject of scrutiny. Suspected or actual lesbian officers faced severe opposition in an organization that strongly emphasizes heterosexual masculine dominance over heterosexual women (Miller, Forest, and Jurik 2004). Women were excluded from after-work socializing. This exclusion disadvantaged women by denying them camaraderie and the informal information needed to excel at work. Women were also excluded from the sponsorship necessary for advancement in highly competitive police organizations (Jurik and Martin 2001). These barriers were commonly faced by women in other traditionally male occupations, including correctional security work, mining, firefighting, and the medical and legal professions (Reskin and Padavic 2002). Policing may be the worst offender because notions of masculinity are so closely associated with the social control functions of police work (Heidensohn 1992).

Even after the 1970s integration period, women continued to face restricted work assignments (Jones 1986). They were disproportionately assigned to clerical and other paperwork duties in the station house while their male counterparts worked the streets, where the most highly regarded police work happened. Even women in supervisory tracts often received assignments that were less prestigious than those given to men counterparts. Evaluations of women were more rigorous and were based on performance standards that emphasized stereotypic masculine qualities like physical and verbal aggressiveness (Martin 1980; Morash and Greene 1986). Thus, policewomen felt pressured to emulate masculine behavior (Brown 2007).

Many policewomen and their supporters responded to such organizational and interpersonal resistance by stressing the unique contribution that so-called feminine traits could offer to police work. Advocates argued that women typically were better communicators than men and that policewomen would be more likely than policemen to diffuse potentially violent conflicts (Martin and Jurik 2007). These arguments resonate with early twentieth-century claims that policewomen were uniquely qualified to work with women and child offenders and victims (Martin 1980). Of course, such arguments may backfire when men devalue skills labeled as uniquely feminine. Despite the limitations posed by gendered stereotypes of policewomen, notions of distinctly feminine skills have at times bolstered women's claims for inclusion and advancement in policing. Since the hiring of women as well as men of color and more highly educated officers was often a response to demands for other changes in police work culture (e.g., community policing, more citizen participation in police governance), hostility to women and men of color was as much a reflection of resentment about these new policies and programs as it was a result of anger about new and more diverse police officers (Jurik and Martin 2001). In recent years, overt hostilities toward policewomen have subsided in many police organizations but have not entirely disappeared. Significant percentages of women officers continue to report problems with blatant resistance and various forms of sexual harassment by male peers. In both the UK and the United States, women are still disproportionately located in junior ranks (Brown and Heidensohn 2000; Silvestri 2003; Martin and Jurik 2007). In the UK, women comprise only about 3 percent of those in supervisory positions. Although most studies suggest that men and women have at least equal aspirations for promotion (Allen 1997; Holdaway and Parker 1998), research also finds that men comprise twice as many applications for promotion to higher ranks on average than women (Scott 1997; Allen 1997).

These interpersonal and organizational impediments to women take a toll with regard to staff retention. Turnover among women continues to be identified as a serious problem in police organizations (Dick and Cassell 2004). Both turnover and advancement limitations among women have been attributed to the conflicting demands of family and paid work. Performance pressures require women to meet and exceed all standards of quality performance. This pressure may leave less time and energy for the double workday that includes caring for home and family.

Although some police organizational changes (e.g., community policing, the caring ethic) facilitated the advancement of women in the 1980s and early 1990s, other, more recent organizational shifts have impeded women's advancements. Budget cuts and increased demands for organizational efficiency have led to reductions in the numbers of staff at higher ranks and thereby increased the work pressures on those in supervisory positions. Marisa Silvestri (2003) attributes such organizational changes to increased demands for 24/7 availability of police supervisors and the erosion of needed flexibility for women with family responsibilities (also see Brown 2003, 2007). Although police officers now officially have access to part-time work arrangements in their agencies, neither women nor men view part-time work or other flexible work arrangements as truly viable for police work. Traditionally masculinist views of policing have not yet been displaced by alternative images that include policewomen (Dick and Cassell 2004). Such organizational changes have exacerbated perceptions that women who have families cannot be viable candidates for promotion (Brown 2007). Susan Martin and Nancy Jurik (2007) identify this form of organizationally embedded disadvantage or "second generation" discrimination as *the* major obstacle to women's advancement in policing and other criminal justice fields in the twenty-first century.

The *Prime Suspect* series has continued through two decades (1991–2006), allowing it to reflect these changes to policewomen as seen through the character of Jane Tennison or, more specifically, in the responses of individuals and of the organization to a high-ranking policewoman. We see a shift from overt hostility to Tennison in earlier episodes to acceptance mingled with more covert and embedded forms of opposition in later episodes. Of course, television programming also has shifted over the years from more restrictive roles for women early on to a wider, more inclusive range of roles today (Lotz 2006). The *Prime Suspect* series is a reflection of cultural transformations and the shifts in television programming aimed to reflect those changes. *Prime Suspect* has also been a catalyst for some of these shifts.

Prime Suspect as a Feminist Police Procedural

The *Prime Suspect* series is an especially interesting phenomenon because it exhibits a number of the traditional elements of police procedurals but also challenges the male-centered nature of the procedural subgenre. Plots not only center on its female lead but also critically convey a sense of the male-dominated structure of police organizations and the struggles of a woman police officer to advance in them. Like other programs in the procedural subgenre, the focus is on the police organization as it tries to discover the identity and procure the arrest of criminals. The protagonist, Jane Tennison, is a detective chief inspector (DCI) of the London Metropolitan Police. By virtue of her rank, she directs a team of detectives in criminal investigations.

Because traditionally procedurals have been resistant to women as lead characters, the *Prime Suspect* series opens the episodes to interesting possibilities that are consistent with a feminist crime genre (see Reddy 1988, 2003). Although the episodes deal with crimes, typically murders, there is less overt violence depicted on-screen, as is often the case in the feminist crime genre (Klein 1992). Moreover, both in character development and in plot, the episodes are relevant to women. Tennison is depicted as a strong-willed character who fights individual and institutional sexism to succeed in her investigations and career.

The *Prime Suspect* series can also be seen as something of a corrective to the more conservative police programs that dominate television. It enjoys a loyal audience in the UK and the United States, especially among professional women (Rennert 1995). In some respects, the series is true to the conventions of the crime genre. It projects a sense of realism that has long been a characteristic of the genre (Krutnik 1991; Thompson 1993). Some critics and scholars (Jermyn 2003; Cavender and Deutsch 2007) argue that it has set a new standard for forensic realism in the procedural subgenre. *Prime Suspect* directors, writers, and actors extensively research the issues in their plots and the actual work of real-life police officers. Some plots are based upon actual cases, and scenes reflect aspects of reality (*Prime Suspect 6* Production Notes, n.d.). In the first film, Tennison, who has been barred from directing any investigations because she is a woman, references an actual survey in which respondents addressed a lack of confidence in women police officers (Smith and Gray 1985). This sense of realism is akin to the police procedural subgenre; those early films in the 1940s often were drawn from actual police investigations, and their presentation featured a documentary-like format (Krutnik 1991; Wilson 2000).

Several scholars argue that television police programs reflect contemporary crises and shifts within actual police organizations as they confront changing social conditions (Reiner 1994; Loader and Mulcahy 2003). Whether such arguments are true of police dramas in general, they are certainly descriptive of the *Prime Suspect* series. *Prime Suspect* episodes convey a sense of the struggles over gender, race, and sexual orientation inequalities within the police organization and how these same inequalities promote tensions between the police and the community. Several episodes consider the ways in which police organizations are progressing (or not progressing) in their internal and external dealings with their diversifying workforce and communities. Episodes in the series depict the implementation of new community policing or public relations strategies; there are references to specialized internal training courses and cultural sensitivity classes. The detectives in the series must do their jobs amid constraints:

they face an often insensitive police hierarchy, external political pressure, and a community that does not trust them. Thus, as a police procedural, the *Prime Suspect* series presents the effort to arrest criminals even as it immerses its audience in the realities of policing in contemporary society.

Prime Suspect's Jane Tennison and Real Policewomen

Tennison's struggle against the male-dominated structure of the London Metropolitan Police is an enduring theme across the *Prime Suspect* episodes. This aspect and the other police procedural elements of the series have been credited with revolutionizing the television crime drama and police procedural subgenre (Sydney-Smith 2007; Jermyn 2010).

Lynda La Plante, creator and screenwriter for *Prime Suspect 1* and *Prime Suspect 3* episodes, has said that she aimed to show the problems of high-ranking policewomen as they existed in the police force during the early 1990s (Day-Lewis 1998). La Plante, a former actress, was inspired by her frustration with the parts for female characters in television—she played a stereotypic prostitute role in one episode of *The Gentle Touch*. She was also influenced by reality television programs and had a penchant for documentary-like film methods of the BBC. Upon learning of the extremely small numbers of women in DCI positions, La Plante undertook the task of learning more about these women's lives. Her research entailed extensive shadowing of the real-life work routines of DCI Jackie Malton, who had experienced considerable problems achieving her own rank (Lambert 1993; McFerran 2006; Day-Lewis 1998, 81–85; Sydney-Smith 2009). La Plante also sought to avoid the more melodramatic style of *Cagney & Lacey*.

Mirren conducted her own research for the series, riding with officers in patrol cars (Sydney-Smith 2009). The portrayal in *Prime Suspect* was so realistic that many of DCI Jackie Malton's friends phoned her after viewing *Prime Suspect 1* and said, "I know it was you; Tennison acted and sounded just like you" (BBC 2004; Lambert 1993). Scholars have commented on the resemblance to the highly publicized legal case of Alison Halford, an assistant chief constable of Merseyside Police who was suspended after trying to achieve promotion (Sydney-Smith 2009). Circulation of such stories further enhanced the sense of verisimilitude associated with the series.

La Plante wrote only one other installment of the series (*Prime Suspect 3*) but did develop the story line for *Prime Suspect 2*; the remaining episodes have been written by men. Regardless, Tennison's struggles against the male-dominated structures of the metropolitan police remain an important theme of the episodes. These ongoing challenges, combined with Tennison's single-minded and hard-driving approach to her job, are consistent with research on the intensification of police management culture in Britain and women's difficulties in advancing to police leadership positions in this increasingly inflexible world (Gaston and Alexander 1997; Silvestri 2003, 2006; Brown 2003, 2007).

Prime Suspect 1 was praised by British policewomen for presenting a realistic portrait of both police work and the discrimination that women have faced entering this male-dominated field; like women in the United States and other nations, British women still struggle to advance to top policing ranks (Westmarland 2001; Brown and Heidensohn 2000; Martin and Jurik 2007).

In 2005 one of us (Jurik) interviewed four women administrators with the London Metropolitan Police, all of whom had worked their way up through the ranks. The narratives of these respondents combined with interview findings reported by other research on British policing (e.g., Silvestri 2003) clearly resonate with much of the portrait of policewomen's experience portrayed in the first six *Prime Suspect* episodes. Respondents stressed that the hazing experienced by women officers at the "Met" was severe, and they were threatened with return to the "beat," that is, street patrol, if they complained. Consistent with the research studies mentioned earlier in this chapter (e.g., Heidensohn 1992; Brown and Heidensohn 2000; Martin and Jurik 2007), respondents described their initial police work experiences as including overt verbal and physical bullying, disrespect, isolation, sabotage, sexualization, and harassment as well as limitations on work assignments and promotional opportunities. Three respondents also praised the later *Prime Suspect* episodes for revealing some of the more organizationally embedded dilemmas for policewomen seeking to advance in the organization.

The dimensions of discrimination experienced by "first-generation" women police officers in the 1980s and 1990s are richly illustrated in the first *Prime Suspect* episode. We detail how Jane Tennison's work life connects to that of real policewomen during this period. First, we present an outline of the plot of *Prime Suspect 1*. (See the Appendix for descriptions of all seven *Prime Suspect* episodes.)

Prime Suspect 1 Plot

The raped and brutally murdered body of a young woman has been discovered, and DCI John Sheffard (John Foregham) is assigned to head the investigation. He hastily identifies the victim as a prostitute who is one of his informants. The prime suspect is George Marlow (John Bowe), whom Sheffard takes into custody without adequate evidence for formal charges. The camaraderie of Sheffard's team, referred to as the "lads," is immediately apparent.

Sheffard suddenly dies of a heart attack, and DCI Jane Tennison asks Detective Chief Superintendent (DCS) Mike Kernan (John Benfield) to give her the case. He calls her timing inappropriate. She persists, noting that for months she has done only paperwork. Kernan's superior orders him to assign Tennison. When the detectives, mostly men, learn of Tennison's assignment, their response is visible disbelief and hostility.

Tennison asks DCS Kernan for the murder case in *Prime Suspect 1*.

Tennison reviews the evidence and concludes that the victim has been misidentified; she was not a prostitute. As Tennison tries to discover the victim's identity, she encounters strong resistance, especially from Detective Sergeant (DS) Bill Otley (Tom Bell), Sheffard's assistant and close friend. Tennison identifies the victim. Then a second victim is discovered; she is the prostitute wrongly identified as the first victim. Lacking evidence, Tennison orders Marlow's release and incurs further hostility from her team. She persists despite resistance and sabotage from subordinates and discovers a similar, earlier murder of a prostitute that occurred north of London. Tennison interviews prostitutes there and discovers that DCI Sheffard also investigated that case. She discovers that Sheffard omitted important information from the official record; she also discovers that he had sex with his prostitute informants. Her discoveries outrage Kernan and Otley, who accuse her of trying to sully Sheffard's reputation.

Three more murdered young women are discovered. Although Tennison released Marlow, she maintains surveillance and pressure on him. DCS Kernan threatens to relieve her for a lack of results. Surprisingly, perhaps because of her persistence, her subordinates request that she remain in charge of the investigation.

Two breaks come simultaneously. Amidst the loud clatter of lads' voices in the squad room, Tennison's policewoman aid, Women's Police Constable (WPC) Maureen Havers (Mossie Smith), quietly notes that the victims were all customers of Marlow's wife, Moyra (Zoë Wanamaker), a manicurist. The detectives follow Marlow to a secret garage that holds his car and grisly evidence of the murders. Moyra recants an alibi that she had provided Marlow. The lads honor Tennison with flowers and champagne. The program ends in the courtroom as Marlow's trial begins and he pleads not guilty.

Prime Suspect 1 and Real Policewomen
in the 1980s and 1990s

Like other police procedurals, *Prime Suspect* depicts both the friendly in-teractions and the seamy side of a police organization. In part what makes the series unique is that the protagonist is a strong woman. She experi-ences sexism, attempted sabotage, and a failed romance, but she solves the murders and wins the respect of the detectives under her supervision. In some respects, the Tennison character resembles her fictional male crime

Tennison gets the assignment.

genre counterparts. She drinks, smokes, curses, and even wears a trench coat. She is aggressive and relentless, and she works long hours sorting evidence and interpreting facts. Ultimately, her persistence pays off: she runs her suspect, Marlow, to ground and earns the respect of the detectives.

Tennison faces obstacles to her leadership and in the investigation, obstacles that are reflective of social science research on women in policing (Westmarland 2001; Brown 2003, 2007; Silvestri 2003). Her experiences comport with the stories of stress and struggle conveyed in our interviews with high-ranking women at the London Metropolitan Police. Like other policewomen who were supposed to be fully integrated into the full range of work opportunities, DCI Tennison finds that getting in is not the same as getting along. She encounters subtle and blatant boundaries throughout her workday. As was the case in the *Juliet Bravo* series, sexism is virtually a taken-for-granted norm in policing. These normative boundaries are visually displayed in the first shot of DCI Tennison in *Prime Suspect 1*. She is barely visible as she is crushed in the back of a crowded elevator. To the degree that the other detectives—all men—notice her at all, it is with an indifferent look. There is an interesting parallel shot in the film *Silence of the Lambs*. Clarice Starling (Jodie Foster) is the only woman in an elevator crowded with FBI men. Whereas Tennison is in the rear, Starling is in the foreground of the elevator shot. Soon we see Tennison and another policewoman in the women's restroom. Their discussion is interrupted when a man detective bursts in and announces that Sheffard is about to break a record (the time from a crime to an arrest). This shot, too, parallels scenes from *Cagney & Lacey* when the women were relegated to their makeshift quarters.

Even though sidelined in the police organization, Tennison knows that every aspect of her performance is carefully scrutinized. She displays a demeanor of confidence and extreme competence, but the camera also shows viewers her private, "backstage" moments of emotion work (see Hochschild 2009). For example, as she approaches DCS Kernan's office to ask for the case after Sheffard's death, Tennison visibly musters her courage. Once in his office, in what seems to be a memorized speech, she tells the DCS, "I'm offering to take over the murder investigation." In a comment that can be read either as bad timing vis-à-vis Sheffard's death or more generally in terms of a woman leading a murder investigation, Kernan responds, "This is not the right time. . . . A man I respected died today. Now's not the time to shove your women's rights down my throat." Kernan's response couches Tennison's request in terms of women's rights, thereby ignoring issues of her competence and the responsibilities typically associated with her rank. The issue becomes "shoving" her "rights" as a woman, not her merit as a competent police DCI.

Tennison references a survey in which 90 percent of the public say they would rather deal with men than with women officers but then adds a further justification for her request, "I'm qualified." She reminds Kernan that for the past eighteen months she has been doing paperwork, not investigating crime. Her dialogue speaks to the role encapsulation that women have confronted trying to break into police work (Martin 1980). Jennifer Hunt (1990) notes that policewomen have often been relegated to administrative paperwork in the station house; it is viewed as "appropriate" feminine labor. Immediately upon Tennison's departure from his office, Kernan begins making phone calls, desperately looking for an available DCI—anyone but Tennison—to replace Sheffard.

A scene follows in which Kernan's superior all but orders him to assign Tennison to the case. The chief says that Tennison's past superiors have reported that she took a lot of punishment coming up through the ranks and suggests that she deserves a break. Kernan laments that such an assignment will be "opening the floodgates" and that "once she is on the case it will be tough to get her off." Clearly, as a token, Tennison represents all policewomen to Kernan and his ilk.

Although placed in charge of the investigation, Tennison is still treated like an outsider. The case is difficult enough, and worse, everyone—subordinates, witnesses, suspects—is disrespectful of her authority. Her detectives are resentful; their facial expressions show dissatisfaction with and inattention to Tennison. DS Otley is the worst of the lot. In a standard sexualization of women criminal justice workers, he calls her a bitch and a tart, always behind her back. He calls her a "dyke-ass" and says, "No bloke would fancy that." In another scene he tries to overhear a phone

Sergeant Otley's anger at Tennison's appointment to head the murder investigation.

conversation to find out who her lover is and charges one of his subordinates to find out about her sex life.

Tennison's public response to men's badgering is professional. When subordinates snidely suggest that she do this or that in the investigation, she agrees that it is a good idea and assigns the task to them. She is capable of directing the efforts of a large team and of tracking down clues herself.

Tennison's strong displays of competence and authority initially threaten her superiors' and subordinates' camaraderie and their identities as men. They continue to closely scrutinize her work and to isolate her through a variety of boundary maintenance activities, that is, interactional strategies that remind women of the differences that separate them from their male colleagues (Kanter 1977). For example, when she views corpses in the morgue and field, the men watch her for signs of faintness. One man cautions her, "It's not a pretty sight," assuming that she will decline to view. Her subordinates display obvious disgust when Tennison unflinchingly examines the body. Her male colleagues are shown either declining to view the bodies or becoming faint when they do.

Typical of women entering all-male occupations, Tennison is denied invitations for after-hours socializing. *Prime Suspect 1* includes a scene where men of all ranks—from detective to the DCS—gather at a men's club to raise money for Sheffard's family. There is drinking, a bawdy comedian, and a boxing match that features DI Frank Burkin (Craig Fairbrass), one of the detectives. Tennison is not a part of the camaraderie; instead, she is appearing on a TV reality crime program trying to solicit clues about the murders. DS Otley leaves his companions and goes to the club bar to watch Tennison on TV. Drunk and agitated, he mutters his recriminations. Kernan joins him, and, as they watch, the DCS realizes that Tennison has made a legal mistake that may allow him to remove her from the case. This scene exemplifies both boundary maintenance and performance pressure on policewomen. It also illustrates the further scrutiny that high-ranking women police face in the news media. The police administrators whom we interviewed cited examples of the intense scrutiny they and other high-ranking women received on the job and in the media.

The close scrutiny of Tennison's performance is reflected in another *Prime Suspect 1* scene. Someone has made a small bureaucratic mistake. DS Otley blames Tennison and urges DCS Kernan to remove her from the case. When Kernan refuses, an irate Otley says, "It's because she's a woman.

If it'd been a bloke . . ." Otley engages in sabotage against Tennison first by hiding information from her and later by bringing in a large group of prostitutes for questioning and blaming Tennison for the resulting station house chaos.

Tennison's response to impediments is not unlike that of classic male detectives; she simply works harder. Visuals depict Tennison analyzing evidence late at night, working long hours to succeed. Similar to fictional male detectives, she exudes a certain emotional detachment when viewing corpses, interviewing suspects, or directing the activities of her subordinates. However, in terms of decentering the traditional emotionless male protagonist, Tennison's lack of emotion is shown to be a facade. After a stressful interview with a suspect or an unsupportive superior, Tennison, once alone, breathes a desperate sigh of relief and, hands shaking, lights a cigarette. As she smokes, her eyes dart this way and that to make sure that she is not being observed by others. Tennison also utilizes women-only spaces to escape the constant scrutiny. In a brief scene, her policewoman assistant finds her eating a sandwich in the women's locker room, avoiding the DCS, who is trying to replace her on the case.

These ongoing challenges, together with Tennison's single-minded and hard-driving approach to her job, are highly consistent with recent studies of the intensification of police management culture in Britain and women's difficulties in advancing to police leadership positions in this increasingly 24/7 world (Gaston and Alexander 1997; Silvestri 2003, 2006). Her life is consistent with the pressures recounted in our own interviews with women police administrators.

The stress and demands of the investigation hurt Tennison's personal life. Her live-in lover, Peter Rawlins (Tom Wilkinson), is initially excited about her assignment, but her absorption in the case and increasing inattention to him take their toll. She succeeds as a DCI, but her devotion to the job comes at the cost of her relationship with Peter. In a series of scenes, he gradually becomes more annoyed by Jane's inattention, her late hours, and the telephone calls from detectives. Peter says, "I hardly ever see you. And when I do . . . what's the point? When the phone rings, I don't exist." Tennison promises, "I'm going to make more time for us soon."

Peter's anger erupts when Tennison, who is supposed to cook dinner for one of his clients, is late; she has been interviewing witnesses and making key discoveries. Peter says, "Just once, I wanted you to do something for me." The next morning, Peter wants to discuss their relationship, but Tennison has to leave for work. On the way to work, her driver says that his wife is complaining about his late hours. Tennison's response is reflective of working women's all too common experience of the double workday: "Yeah, at least you go home and you get your dinner cooked. When I go home, I have to cook it myself."

When Tennison gets home that night, Peter has moved out. As she reads his good-bye note, she listens to her mom's phone message that her sister has had a baby. This aspect of the narrative suggests that women must choose between career success and family—at least if they seek success as a high-level police official.

Second-Generation Discrimination

The women police administrators at the London Met with whom we spoke agreed that circumstances for women in policing have improved markedly since the 1980s and early 1990s. However, they uniformly stressed that work/life balance continues to be a major problem for women working in policing. Much overt resistance to women has "gone underground," as they called it. In some stations there is still open hostility, but most issues for women now revolve around the lack of flexibility available to women seeking to combine motherhood and a policing career. Even though family leave policies and part-time work arrangements exist formally within the police organization, informally these policies are not always well implemented.

Later *Prime Suspect* episodes reveal embedded gender disadvantages and the long-term consequences of Tennison's struggles to succeed. She continues to battle the male buddy system, which covers up occasions of police corruption and wrongdoing (e.g., *Prime Suspect 3*, *Prime Suspect 5: Errors of Judgment*). As she mentors other, younger policewomen, she often suspects that they might be undermining or betraying her to hostile and competitive male colleagues (e.g., *Prime Suspect 4*: "Inner Circles," *Prime Suspect 5: Errors of Judgment*). Tennison's exposure of police corruption, enhanced visibility as a woman, and exclusion from the friendship networks of male peers and superiors converge to disadvantage her for promotion and choice assignments (e.g., *Prime Suspect 2*). In *Prime Suspect 6: The Last Witness*, Tennison is a bit envious of and even negative toward a female subordinate who has young children and who has been able to take advantage of more recently implemented department policies prohibiting overt discrimination against mothers. We also see Tennison's heightened sense of paranoia and problematic drinking in response to these pressures and her lack of enduring personal relationships in *Prime Suspect 7: The Final Act*.

Conclusion

Historically, policing existed without women as personnel in important positions. The crime genre—in novels and on television—was largely devoid of women protagonists. This absence changed beginning in the 1970s as, more than ever before, women entered the professional workforce, including the ranks of the police.

The *Prime Suspect* series changed the landscape by introducing a feminist-inspired television crime series and DCI Jane Tennison, a compelling character who investigates murders even as she confronts the myriad problems of contemporary policing. The series offers a close look at police routines and at life in the police organization, a social institution that must change as society changes.

The iconic figure of Jane Tennison and the powerful procedural series exemplify the assertion that the increasing presence of women is so significant that it constitutes a new genre, a feminist crime genre (Reddy 1988; Klein 1992; Sydney-Smith 2003). The realism of the series includes surprisingly accurate and detailed portraits of the barriers faced by real-life policewomen in the 1980s and 1990s. Consistent with our model of progressive moral fiction, the series offers insights into the experiences of women as a socially marginalized group in policing. Their struggles are very much located within the larger societal and organizational (i.e., structural) context of policing. *Prime Suspect 1* reveals Tennison's triumph in overcoming opposition to her appointment and in solving the case. Accordingly, it offers glimpses of success that women can have in the workplace, perhaps inciting and providing an inspiration for social change. Later episodes reveal her struggles and successes and illustrate the continuation of overt and organizationally embedded resistance to women in the still male-dominated world of policing. Women officer/administrators from the London Met said that the *Prime Suspect* series offered a realistic portrayal of their struggles to make it in policing.

Also consistent with our model, *Prime Suspect* extends its procedural realism in its portraits of the larger social context of crimes and police/

community tensions. We will discuss this aspect of the program as progressive moral fiction in Chapter 5.

Despite these positive elements, the series shows the limitations of work in police organizations, especially problems for women, as well as the issues of doing justice in policing. It reveals issues of work/life balance for a working woman, problems that Tennison seems never to successfully address. We will further discuss these issues in later chapters, but next we turn to Tennison's methods of detection.

CHAPTER 3

Investigating and Challenging

In this chapter we consider both the strategies of detection that enable Jane Tennison to solve cases and the television production techniques employed in the series that establish Tennison as a credible and successful female protagonist in a previously male-dominated subgenre. Thus, we examine methods whereby the male dominance of the police procedural is decentered in *Prime Suspect*.

To attract an audience, authors and creators of new crime genre productions typically distinguish their chief protagonist with some unique personality characteristics or detecting method. The *Prime Suspect* series combines realism with the highly competent, driving force of a woman succeeding in what has been very much a man's world. In order to solve cases, Tennison must constantly overcome gender barriers in her police work setting. She challenges organizational and interpersonal barriers to successfully perform her job. In conducting investigations, she demonstrates a relentless work ethic and aggressiveness, close attention to case details and forensic evidence, some occasional duplicity, and what appear to be special "feminine" insights. We argue that Tennison's careerism and desire for justice drive her investigations.

A central component of the crime genre is the methodology for solving the crime and identifying the villain(s) who committed it. Klein (1992) identifies three key elements of this genre as the crime, the detective, and the quest. The pleasures of the crime genre include not only the effort to figure out whodunit but also watching the detective as he or she investigates and solves the crime (Cawleti 1976). Accordingly, crime genre productions devote a lot of attention to the detective's methods and character. We will add to this list the consideration of production techniques whereby the detectives' methods and character are conveyed.

Initially, the crime genre focused on amateur and private detectives. In the early days of the genre (the 1800s), C. Auguste Dupin and Sherlock Holmes were portrayed as masters of ratiocination. Their creators, Edgar Allan Poe and Sir Arthur Conan Doyle, depicted them in many scenes simply thinking. Doyle also provided a wealth of detail about Holmes's personality, his eccentricities, and his methods. These somewhat bourgeois private investigators were able to solve cases that eluded their working-class counterparts in the police; sometimes these master thinkers were critical of the police. Later (1920 through the 1930s), Miss Marple used reasoned insights about people derived from years of village life in order to solve cases that baffled the police.

Private detectives Sam Spade and Philip Marlowe in the 1930s and 1940s were men of action. Often depicted as literally clueless, they nonetheless solved crimes because of their relentless investigations. These hard-boiled variants of the crime genre offered more action than the reason-centered cozy productions: protagonists were warned off cases, fired, and beaten, but they refused to quit.

Although there had always been police characters in the crime genre, they became a focal point when the police procedural subgenre emerged in the 1940s. The police procedural centered on police work routines and teamwork in novels like Lawrence Treat's *V as in Victim* (1945) and in films like *The Naked City* (1948). Those earlier, more realistic procedurals were followed decades later by "fantasy procedurals." Television procedurals such as *Z Cars* and *The Sweeney*, discussed in the Introduction, featured action and adventure mixed with police routines. These fantasy realism productions sought to portray both the realities of tough streets and action-adventure police heroes (Sydney-Smith 2007).

Prime Suspect presents a more realistic sense of police routines and also some notion of the interpersonal and organizational dynamics surrounding police work. Ultimately, the series conveys a sense of the grueling work regimes required to yield solutions to a crime. At times, Tennison appears to have special "feminine" insights; however, she is always shown working hard to solve the crime and stay ahead of supervisors and subordinates who do not think she can do it.

Prime Suspect production techniques present a new method or "politics" of looking. In later sections of this chapter, we discuss narrative, mise-en-scène, and other production techniques that decenter the masculine vantage point and domination of the procedural subgenre.

Unique Dimensions of *Prime Suspect*

Prime Suspect represents an interesting take on the police drama. The series is a police procedural, especially in its depiction of the details of police work. The detectives are depicted in various routine activities that embody aspects of contemporary policing: canvassing neighborhoods, interviewing witnesses, reviewing bank records, attending training sessions, and conducting crime scene investigations. Many of the scenes are based on research and consultation about actual police work because accuracy enhances the verisimilitude of the police procedural for audiences that have increasingly more knowledge about police operations (Dove 1982).

Even though *Prime Suspect* is a police procedural, it also is star-driven drama because of Dame Helen Mirren's portrayal of Jane Tennison. The series devotes attention both to Tennison as a character and to her methods of detection. We see the case and the quest to solve it from her perspective. We also see Tennison as a woman faced with a problem that Klein (1992) argues is more frequently confronted in a feminist crime genre: whether or not to trust the patriarchal criminal justice system. At each stage she must approach her police colleagues with caution. Part of the suspense associated with Tennison's quest is whether she can prove that she can do the job and overcome the hurdles that her team and the police hierarchy lay in her path. The series is also suggestive of the special skills and insights that she brings to her cases as a woman. Such special talents have been often discussed in literature about women working in traditionally male criminal justice fields, although the validity of such claims and the degree to which unique talents attributed to women serve to advance women's equality in these fields are matters of some debate (Brown and Heidensohn 2000; Martin and Jurik 2007).

As noted in Chapter 2, *Prime Suspect* incorporates scientific and particularly forensic methods of crime detection (Jermyn 2003). Although Sherlock Holmes is often depicted as simply thinking, these stories and later film and television renditions also portray him as a pioneer in the use of scientific detection methods. Holmes was aware of fingerprint technology, he experimented with chemical analysis, and he was conversant with scientific knowledge about crime and criminals (Harrington 2007). Most of Holmes's successors did not incorporate his scientific methodology into their investigations. For example, 1960s and 1970s detective and police television series featured detectives who relied on their wits and fists to trap criminals. There were a few exceptions. *Quincy* (1976–83), a US television program series that featured a pathologist who worked for the Los Angeles County coroner's office, directed attention to the forensics surrounding the police autopsy. Television's forensic concerns were unusual prior to the *Prime Suspect* series.

In *Prime Suspect* episodes, once a body is discovered, a crime scene investigation ensues. Tennison arrives on the scene as experts busily gather forensic evidence. An autopsy scene, also with Tennison in attendance, often follows. These scenes offer close-up views of the corpse as the coroner details the condition of the body and likely cause of death. Throughout the rest of the episode, the murder investigation team under Tennison's supervision not only gathers evidence but waits for and considers reports from the experts.

Tennison ponders the broken skull of a murder victim.

Tennison's investigative team also relies on a variety of other scientific and technological crime detection strategies. Computerized checks of bank records, car registrations, and housing occupancy are routine in *Prime Suspect* investigations. In most episodes, she assigns a member of her squad to scrutinize the CCTV tapes of the crime scene or other relevant locations. In *Prime Suspect 2* the investigation is focused on the murder of a young woman whose body is decomposed. In order to facilitate identification of the victim, Tennison commissions the construction of a bust of the victim based on the forensic analysis of her skeleton. These examples illustrate the variety of techniques and experts that may be used in police routines, and they have become a convention in the police drama. Indeed, they generated a new subgenre, the forensic police drama, which includes *CSI* (2000–), *Bones* (2005–), and *Silent Witness* (1996–).

Performance Pressures and "Special" Insights

Even though Tennison directs a team of detectives, a recurrent theme in the series is her own attention to detail and hard work, work that shows her awake at all hours, tediously examining case materials. In *Prime Suspect 5: Errors of Judgment* she describes her methodology to a subordinate: "Listen, Clare, I only know one way to work, and that's through instinct and slog." In *Prime Suspect 1*, fairly certain of Marlow's guilt, she relentlessly pursues clues that implicate him; she plans an elaborate surveillance that tracks Marlow to his secret garage. In *Prime Suspect 4*: "Scent of Darkness," more Marlow-like murders occur. Since Marlow is in prison, Tennison's superiors decide that she botched the original case. She is removed from the investigation of the new murders but, nevertheless, doggedly pursues the case in order to vindicate her reputation and track down the real killer. Interviews with real women in policing suggest that the heightened scrutiny of policewomen makes them feel vulnerable to frequent allegations of botched casework and negative media publicity (Silvestri 2003; Martin and Jurik 2007). Thus, although Tennison's relentless pursuit in *Prime Suspect 4*: "Scent of Darkness," is fictional, the story line resonated with the past experiences of our respondents who were real policewomen.

In other respects, Tennison reinforces the notion that a woman detective may have unique skills in gathering and interpreting evidence. Reminiscent of a short film entitled *A Jury of Her Peers* (1980), in which women

While interviewing prostitutes, Tennison herself is approached by a would-be client.

solve a mystery because they see clues that men cannot see, Tennison sees clues that men detectives miss. These unique insights are especially pronounced in *Prime Suspect 1*. After carefully examining the clothing and personal effects of the victim, Tennison realizes that she has been wrongly identified. The victim, supposedly a prostitute, was dressed in "boutique clothes," and Tennison quickly notes that her shoes did not match the shoe size recorded for the alleged victim. Once she views the body, Tennison realizes that the homicide victim bears little resemblance to the photo of the missing prostitute who was misidentified as the victim. Tennison then travels north of London and locates prostitutes who were friends of the woman who was originally thought to be the victim. She buys them a drink in a pub, and, unlike her male colleagues, she actually listens to these women. When a man propositions her, Tennison does not distance herself from the prostitutes. Instead she simply says, "I'm busy right now. Sod off!" The women are amused by this and pleased by her ease with and respectful treatment of them; they provide her with important information that was missing from the official record because no one interviewed them. She gives them voice and credence.

A final example of "special womanly" insights comes from WPC Maureen Havers, Tennison's policewoman assistant who discovers the link among the victims. Havers's insight actually cracks the case, but when she tries to explain it, the men in the room are too loud and do not listen to her. Tennison asks everyone to be quiet. Havers begins to explain how, despite his denials, Marlow did know the victims. The detectives are still too loud; Tennison again asks for quiet. The detectives take little heed of Tennison and Havers, who sit in the middle of the room. Tennison listens patiently as Havers quietly explains the missing link that has eluded everyone else. Marlow's wife, Moyra, did the victims' nails—a link that men would miss. These examples confirm Reddy's (1988) observations about fictional women detectives as well other arguments that real policewomen can offer unique skills and insights to the job (Martin and Jurik 2007).

Although claims of special feminine talents smack of gender essentialism, Tennison's unique insights can also be located in gender-related but not gender-determined factors: her performance pressure and marginalized

Tennison working late.

social status. First, knowing her performance will be carefully scrutinized, Tennison works very hard, tends to detail, and seems to miss nothing. In *Prime Suspect 1*, after her assignment to the case, Tennison immediately requests that all records and evidence be brought to her for reanalysis. It is her thorough review of evidence that yields the information about clothing and the prior misidentification of the victim. Second, as a woman, Tennison is herself an organizational outsider. Also, because she is a highly motivated working woman in a demanding and male-dominated occupation, she is an outsider to segments of society that continue to hold traditional views about women's roles both at work and in family life. It is not surprising that throughout the *Prime Suspect* series she often relates better to witnesses and victims who are socially marginalized than to her male colleagues. Her marginalized status and consequent performance pressures converge to inspire Tennison to think outside the organizational box. Ultimately, her "special" insights likely derive more from her social and organizational status as a woman rather than from her genetic composition; her lived experiences facilitate her willingness to see.

In these contexts Tennison also exhibits traits associated with a more caring orientation toward policing (Reiner 1994). Klein (1992) argues that an ethic of care is associated with protagonists in the feminist crime genre. In fact, there were already elements of the caring style reflected in *Prime Suspect* forerunners *Dixon of Dock Green, The Gentle Touch*, and *Juliet Bravo*.

Overcoming Hurdles

Although it can be argued that much of Tennison's behavior is consistent with an ethic of care toward victims and witnesses, it is nevertheless the case that much of Tennison's behavior is aggressive and relentless toward her police subordinates and superiors and sometimes quite duplicitous toward members of the community. This dimension of Tennison's character has led some scholars to label her character masculinist and an anathema to a feminist crime genre (Brooks 1994; Jermyn 2003). Ironically, her commanding behavior must also be understood as essential to life in a hierarchical organization; it might not be questioned were she a man. Rather than categorizing her behavior as either feminist or masculinist, or either good or bad, we wish to address the degree to which her persona actually complicates and destabilizes traditional notions of gender identities and of who can police.

Tennison does not hesitate to challenge and reprimand subordinates who block her progress on a case either intentionally through sabotage or unintentionally through inadequate work performance. When she first takes charge of the team in *Prime Suspect 1*, DS Otley angrily confronts her, saying, "Look, I know you asked for this case specifically . . ." Tennison cuts him off, saying, "If you don't like it, put in for a transfer, and it will be dealt with by the normal channels." She stares at the men, pauses a moment, and asks: "Anyone else?" Later, in *Prime Suspect 5: Errors of Judgment*, Tennison grows impatient with the failure of her team to make progress on the case. In response to a vague answer from a subordinate, she irately exclaims, "Oh come on, you lot! Let's just be a bit precise about this! Okay? . . . Well it's official. Things are not going well!" On her way out of the room, she slams a file drawer shut.

With superiors who block either her case or her career progress Tennison is equally assertive to the point of aggressiveness. Sometimes her actions border on insubordination. In *Prime Suspect 1*, when her superior, DCS Mike Kernan, promises Tennison that he will think about assigning her to a case, she says, "Well, that's just not enough, Mike." Reading his angry expression, she reins herself in and exits his office. She has another run-in with Kernan in *Prime Suspect 2*. Tennison and Kernan argue when she learns that he has assigned DS Bob Oswalde (Colin Salmon) to her team without discussing the action with her. An angry Tennison responds, "Oh bollocks," then collects herself and adds, "Sir." In several episodes (*Prime Suspect 4*: "Scent of Darkness," *Prime Suspect 6: The Last Witness*, and *Prime Suspect 7: The Final Act*) Tennison is ordered to drop a case or to avoid any contact with specific witnesses. In each case she persists, usually with the aid of a loyal subordinate, and, despite orders, produces the killer. In *Prime Suspect 6: The Last Witness* she disobeys a direct order not to travel to Bosnia. Tennison goes to Bosnia and, when she phones in reports, lies about her whereabouts.

Tennison's relentless style also sometimes includes deception of witnesses and suspects. In *Prime Suspect 2* she interviews witness David Harvey (Tom Watson) on his deathbed. Tennison suspects that Harvey, who lived next door to the victim, has withheld information about the case. Tennison tells Harvey, who is a Catholic, that she, too, is Catholic and knows that he might want to unburden himself before he dies. In the same episode Tennison tries to bond with another witness, Sarah Allen (Jenny Jules), in order to gain important information from her.

In *Prime Suspect 6: The Last Witness* Tennison cleverly reveals a husband's infidelity to his wife. The husband is a suspect in a double murder. In anger, the wife offers incriminating information about her husband, which Tennison secretly tape-records. Later, Tennison plays the tape for the husband's accomplice, who angrily reveals another murder and the location of the body.

Tennison's deceitful actions are replicated in a number of other police dramas in which police officers use a variety of deceits to obtain confessions, for example, *NYPD Blue* (1993–2005) and *The Closer* (2005–) These fictional depictions actually parallel the strategies and practices of real police detectives, who are not required to tell the truth during interviews or interrogations.

Tennison's relentless work ethic extends to an almost total subsumption of her private life into her work. In several episodes she draws on the expertise of lovers or former lovers to help with a case. In *Prime Suspect 3* she meets with Jake Hunter (Michael Shannon), a successful author and criminal profiler who is a former lover. Hunter wants to rekindle their old romance. After Tennison rebuffs his overtures, she asks for his help on a case. In *Prime Suspect 4: "The Lost Child,"* she meets with Dr. Patrick Schofield (Stuart Wilson), a psychiatrist who treated a suspect in her child molestation case. Tennison and Schofield become lovers, and in *Prime Suspect 4: "Scent of Darkness,"* she consults him in the Marlow copycat murders.

Thus far we have focused on Tennison's methods of detection—hard work and the relentless pursuit of a solution to her cases. She sometimes exhibits seemingly "feminine" insights and an ethic of caring, but these must also be viewed within the context of her dogged determination to overcome obstacles and solve the crime. She is not above deceit and use of spurned lovers to achieve this goal. In many respects, these are typical traits associated with the quests of private and police detectives. However, we argue in the next section that the narratives and mise-en-scène of *Prime Suspect* go beyond "business as usual" to more fundamentally disrupt the masculine procedural subgenre.

Disrupting the Genre: A New Politics of Looking

A key component of the quest in the crime genre is a detective's close observation of people and evidence. Indeed, the crime genre is all about seeing; it foregrounds the act of looking. The detective sees and deduces what others miss (Walton and Jones 1999, 157; Mizejewski 2004, 7; Jermyn 2003). In the case of television, the camera is the vehicle for seeing.

As noted, the audience derives pleasure from watching the detective's investigation. However, feminist critics of the genre argue that traditionally there has been a problematic aspect of watching the male detective. Because the audience is forced to take a heterosexual male perspective through either the writer's or the camera's eye, it must derive pleasure (scopophilia) by looking at women's bodies. The body is a central feature of these stories: a corpse motivates the action; it not only symbolizes a serious threat to the social order (Mizejewski 2004, 14) but also conveys a set of established meanings—that men are dominant and women are passive—as well as a vocabulary of violence against women (Walkowitz 1982, 545; Wykes and Gunter 2005, 39). Autopsy scenes are especially problematic in the traditional genre. The victim, already brutalized, is further mutilated and opened up to perusal by men who speak in the cold, detached language of policing and medicine. A woman investigator disrupts the conventions of the traditionally male genre. She produces "a new politics of looking" (see Cavender and Jurik 2007; Sydney-Smith 2009).

However, we argue that in *Prime Suspect* the disruption of the traditional manner in which crime genre television and film "look" at women goes beyond the mere presence of a woman detective (Cavender and Jurik 2007). The disruption extends through both the scripts and the scene composition (mise-en-scène) utilized in the series. Disruption is evident in the relative naturalness of Tennison's interactions with other women, such as her scene with prostitutes in *Prime Suspect 1* discussed earlier. In *Prime Suspect 4*: "The Lost Child," the energy that drives the episode comes from the fact that Tennison, who has just terminated her own pregnancy, comes to the aid of a mother whose child appears to have been kidnapped. Tennison's connection to this mother is clearly an emotional one: she gave up her opportunity to become a mother but dedicates herself to finding this mother's child. The episode conveys both the pleasures and the hardships associated with motherhood in our contemporary world, a world that requires women to both earn a living and nurture their children.

Prime Suspect is perhaps at its most disruptive of genre conventions in the scenes in which Tennison looks at murdered women's bodies at crime scenes or autopsies. In *Prime Suspect 1* her male colleagues first organizationally—by refusing her assignment to a murder case—and then later literally try to keep her away from the bodies of the victims. Once on the case, when she asks to see the body of a victim, DS Eastel (Dave Bond) physically blocks her for a moment and verbally discourages her by saying, "It isn't a pretty sight." Tennison responds, "I want to see her." Camera shots frame Tennison in close proximity with women victims. She is professional but also respectful; it is as if this close proximity allows her to draw something from these women, not in the almost supernatural sense of the woman pathologist character, Sam Ryan, in the television program *Silent Witness* (1996–), but still something that is deep and fundamental. The closeness seems to motivate Tennison to seek justice for the women in a manner consistent with Klein's (1992) portrait of the feminist crime genre. In contrast, it is her male colleagues who are shown wincing or becoming ill at the sight of women victims' dead bodies.

Contrast such scenes with those in other productions in which male detectives make disrespectful wisecracks as they view the naked bodies of murdered women or in which crotchety medical examiners ply their trade while enjoying lunch. For example, in the film *Blink*, Detective John Hallstrom (Aidan Quinn) has a faux conversation with a murdered woman whose naked body is lying in a bathtub: he sarcastically demands that she tell him who killed her.

Mise-en-Scène and *Prime Suspect 6: The Last Witness*

In order to further illustrate the manner in which the scene composition of *Prime Suspect* is interwoven with the plot narrative so as to connect Tennison with the victims, we draw several examples from an analysis of *Prime Suspect 6: The Last Witness*. In Cavender and Jurik (2007) we analyze the ways in which this episode challenges traditional and male-centered police subgenre scene composition. The episode centers on Tennison's search for the killer of two Bosnian refugees, sisters Samira and Jasmina

Blekic, who escaped ethnic cleansing in Bosnia. The political establishment and the police are anti-immigrant in their comments. Tennison's growing awareness of the plight of refugees is revealed in both dialogue and scene composition.

Beginning with the autopsy scene in *Prime Suspect 6: The Last Witness*, we see Tennison draw close to the body of the victim, Samira Blekic, as the medical examiner describes her torture and murder. Despite the gory nature of some of the camera shots that accompany the autopsy, the audience sees Samira from Tennison's perspective. Tennison moves very close to the body in an obviously inquisitive manner. However, in addition to her professional interest in the body, Tennison is obviously touched by Samira, remarking, "She was very beautiful." Enhanced by the sound track and the soft tone of the dialogue, the scene takes on a respectful, almost reverential quality and contemplation on the part of the woman medical examiner (Leena Dhingra) and Tennison about what Samira might have been like in life. Again in contrast, the other detectives, mostly men, are separated from the surgical theater, separated from the victim's body. Some of them are visibly ill. It is almost as if the scene is composed around Tennison, the medical examiner, Samira, and the audience.

This autopsy scene roughly parallels a previous scene in the same episode where Tennison is on an examination table undergoing her annual physical. Similar camera angles in the two scenes—trained first on Jane Tennison and later on Samira Blekic—as well as the general situation of a passive female body being subjected to the intrusion of a medical examination create the parallel. Moreover, Tennison's physical examination immediately follows the scene wherein Samira's body is discovered, initially adding at least a brief possibility that it is the murder victim's body, not Tennison's, that is being examined.

Indeed, throughout *Prime Suspect 6: The Last Witness*, scene composition often places Tennison's body in rough parallels to the bodies of the Blekic sisters. The mise-en-scène conveys a sense of Tennison's empathy and commitment to justice for the murdered sisters. And, of course, these scenes disrupt the usual male gaze that is common in the traditional crime genre. For example, after Tennison discovers Jasmina Blekic (Ingeborga Dapkūnaitė), who is hiding in a compartment beneath the floor, a scene follows in which Tennison tries to calm her, to win her confidence, and to gain information that might help with the investigation of Samira's murder. The composition of the scene locates both Tennison and Jasmina on a couch; they are seated in parallel postures. In a close-up shot, Jasmina leans forward, knees together and hands clasped, a body language that reflects grief and fear. A wider shot then reveals Tennison in almost the same posture: her knees and hands parallel Jasmina's posture. A series of close-up shots follows in which Tennison either leans forward and looks at Jasmina in profile or looks downward, as if searching for words even as she respects Jasmina's grief and fear. The camera angle is level with the two women and usually includes both of them in the frame as it alternates between objective shots with first Jasmina and then Tennison in the foreground. Given our earlier comments about Tennison's sometimes deceitful interrogation techniques, her posture could be interpreted as a strategy. However, the framing of their parallel postures also suggests a connection between the two women (Adelman, Cavender, and Jurik 2009).

Jasmina does gradually open up to Tennison and, in a series of interviews, shares the details of the brutal rape and torture that she and her

Tennison interviews a frightened Jasmina Blekic, whom she has just discovered hiding under the floor.

sister suffered eleven years earlier at the hands of Dragon Yankovic. Interestingly, one of these scenes between Tennison and Jasmina takes place in the women's restroom. Like several scenes in *Prime Suspect 1*, this is a place that Tennison and other women can go to escape the intrusion of men. She is able to get Jasmina to open up to her but cannot prevent Jasmina's eventual murder by Yankovic. Afterward, Tennison so aggressively pursues the murderer that she risks her own career.

A later scene exhibits another parallel between Tennison's body and the bodies of the Blekic sisters. After she has begun to suspect that Milan Lukic, the optician and part-time police interpreter, is involved in Samira Blekic's murder, Tennison goes to him ostensibly for an eye examination but also to gather information. This highly charged scene depicts a seemingly innocuous examination that is really a tense confrontation between Tennison and a dangerous, sadistic man. As the examination begins, in close-up, the camera follows Lukic (Oleg Men'shikov) as he rolls his chair toward Tennison and subtly slides his knee between her knees. He tells her that this is to facilitate the examination, but his movements are an intrusive violation of her personal space. During a scene that is also shot in extreme close-up, Lukic causes Tennison pain as he examines her eyelids. His demeanor during the examination is imperial—as the optician, he is in control—and menacing. Later, in Bosnia, Tennison learns that Milan Lukic is really an alias for a paramilitary commander named Dragon Yankovic who directed the murder of Bosnian Muslims and personally tortured the Blekic sisters. Obviously, Yankovic/Lukic's treatment of Tennison is not as severe as his torture of the Blekic sisters, but there is a parallel in the mise-en-scène of the examination sequence. Yankovic/Lukic's intruding knee is of a sexual nature and an unwanted physical intrusion that asserts his power. He is nonchalant about the pain he causes Tennison as he examines her eyelids in much the same way as he was unconcerned about torturing Samira or raping Jasmina.

While the mise-en-scène of the eye examination parallels the situation of the Blekic sisters, there are important differences. The act of looking is Tennison's act: subjective camera shots often take her perspective. So although the examination is unpleasant and Lukic's behavior disconcerting, the camera (and audience) experiences it from Tennison's point of view. Also, unlike the sisters, who were vulnerable victims, Tennison is more in control. Her questions make Lukic the object of her investigation. She subjects herself to Yankovic/Lukic's examination as a part of her quest to catch a killer.

The final scene that we will detail from *Prime Suspect 6: The Last Witness* includes a sequence of Tennison in Bosnia. She travels there because of a video of the atrocity that Jasmina has described to her, an atrocity that is denied by MI6. In an objective shot, the camera shows Tennison in an empty Quonset hut–type building looking at the bullet-riddled wall against which the Muslims were killed. Next, in a series of shots that alternate between objective shots in which we see Tennison staring through the empty building and subjective shots in which we see what she saw in the video, we view the aftermath of the atrocity as family and friends (mostly women) of the victims enter the building. They are weeping and wringing their hands in grief as they approach a pile of bloody bodies. The devastation of the survivors as they kneel beside the bodies conveys the horrors of war, all the more horrible because MI6 denied that the atrocity had occurred. Overcome, Tennison exits the building with a painful look on her face. Like the survivors, she cannot stand; she slumps down onto a bench. Again the mise-en-scène has placed Tennison's body where the bodies of the victims and the survivors experienced these horrors years before. As in the eye examination, Tennison not only sees what happened but will act to seek justice, at least for the Blekic sisters.

After Yankovic is arrested for the real Lukic's murder, Tennison remains in his backyard for a moment. In this last scene of the episode, she appears overcome with sadness and reflection, perhaps giving the audience time to reflect on the drama of the case and the loss of the Blekic sisters and other victims in the atrocities of war.

Conclusion

In the past the crime genre has emphasized the detective's personality and focused on *his* detecting methods. *Prime Suspect* follows some of these conventions as it reveals Tennison's ambition and drive and her management of a team in the routines of the police procedural. Her methods of detection are comprised of intuition and slogging as well as some apparently womanly insights, but she also evidences a relentless and aggressive work ethic. She sometimes employs deceit in her investigations, and she stands up for herself, sometimes almost to the point of insubordination.

Although *Prime Suspect* breaks new ground for realism in its vivid autopsy scenes, these scenes also markedly disrupt the conventions of the traditionally male-centric genre. If the genre foregrounds the act of looking (Jermyn 2003), it is DCI Jane Tennison, a woman, who is looking. Tennison looks with a unique sensibility at other women and at those who are socially marginalized. Her demeanor in these instances sharply contrasts with the humorous and disrespectful tone that is common in many police dramas. As we have demonstrated, the mise-en-scène often includes Tennison's body in settings and postures that evoke empathy with the women and others whom she encounters in her investigations. Even though she is a police detective, Jane Tennison posits a different view of a crime genre protagonist's answer to the somewhat ideological questions, What is justice, and whose side are we on? We address these matters in the next chapters.

CHAPTER 4

Doing Justice

The crime genre offers a template for examining collective anxieties and issues of justice (Brunsdon 2000). Television crime productions generally, and police procedurals in particular, typically adopt quite narrow definitions of law, order, and justice. The definitions of justice have become so narrow in many recent productions that the law-and-order concept actually implies a disregard of law whenever it is necessary for police to catch criminals. Criminals in such productions are portrayed in one-dimensional and stereotypical fashions as embodiments of evil, even if it is below the surface of otherwise normal appearances. Individual responsibility for wrongdoing is stressed without serious attention to real-world social issues and contexts that might generate such criminal actions. Only the police can contain the violence and keep it away from law-abiding middle- and upper-class communities. Still, we wish to consider possibilities wherein novels, films, and television can use the crime genre as a means to address social issues and challenge conventional notions of justice.

Drawing on our model of progressive moral fiction outlined in Chapter 1, we suggest that protagonists within progressive moral fictional works operate as justice provocateurs to question and challenge narrow notions of justice as law and order and restoring the status quo. As we have noted, several scholars (Klein 1992, 49–50; Munt 1994; Klein 1995, 215; Reddy 2003) suggest that works within a feminist crime genre also challenge limited notions of justice typically contained in crime genre productions.

In this chapter we are interested specifically in *Prime Suspect*'s treatment of justice issues. The question for us is the degree to which *Prime Suspect* fits within the corpus of a feminist crime genre and embodies a commitment to the tenets of a progressive moral fiction. We consider Jane Tennison's role as a justice provocateur. Do the series and its chief protagonist merely reinforce restoration of the status quo, or do they convey a sense of the limits of law and the criminal justice system, of the fissures in societal and police organizational power structures? And to what extent, if any, is *Prime Suspect* imagery empowering with regard to individual or collective opportunities for promoting social justice or social transformation?

We turn next to a discussion of the importance of studying the crime genre and the ideological nature of most works in this realm. After this review, we direct our attention to the analysis of justice in specific *Prime Suspect* episodes and in the series more generally. In this analysis we closely attend to both implicit and explicit messages related to justice in procedural and substantive forms. We will present examples of action and dialogue that exemplify Jane Tennison as a justice provocateur. We then turn to a discussion of the limitations of the doing of justice by Jane Tennison and in the series as a whole.

The Significance and Ideology of the Crime Genre

Cain killed Abel. If it bleeds, it leads. These two simple, declarative statements, one that is part of an origin myth about humanity and the other a description of the news media's penchant for violence, reflect our fascination with crime. There is a paradox in this: we delight in tales that put us in a state of suspense or scare us, show rules being broken and people being killed, show threats to the social order, and yet in the denouement of such tales we enjoy a resolution that restores order and produces a sense of justice. Ever since Abel's murder and Cain's banishment for fratricide, crime has been a theme in many popular stories.

Thus, the crime genre offers considerable insight into the values and meanings held by a society at any given time. It can also be an important disseminator of images about crime, including its causes and perpetrators, and of meanings of justice. Lenz (2003) suggests that we should pay close attention to crime stories. Most people have no firsthand knowledge about crime, so crime news and, equally important, crime stories shape our thinking about crime and justice (also see Savelsberg 1994). Crime stories help to establish an agenda for how we define crime, for whom we see as the criminal, and for the "just" solutions that we consider when redressing crime. These stories contain the paradox that we mentioned above, but because of our antipathy to crime, they also represent a sort of "time out" in terms of how we usually think about social issues. For example, a common expectation of news media is that they offer balanced coverage of social issues. Few would expect even a pretense of balance when news media cover crime: victims are usually depicted as innocent people, and criminals are depicted as bad people who deserve punishment. In the abstract, most of us would not define as a happy ending one wherein a fictional hero hurts or kills other characters, but we do accept—some say we demand—such endings in the crime genre. By condemning criminals, the denouement of crime stories functions in an almost Durkheimian manner to restore the social order that is disrupted by criminals and to condemn them for that disruption (Schattenberg 1981).

The crime genre has always been ideological both in form (traditionally appealing to particular views of realism defined in terms of empirical and rational methods) and in content. The selection of the crimes and criminals addressed identifies who and what threaten society and what constitutes social order (Knight 1980). For example, even *The Newgate Calendar*, which reportedly began the crime genre (discussed in the Introduction), conveyed ideological messages.

These ideological messages are obscured by the seemingly innocuous form of a popular genre, by its formulaic repetition, and by its happy endings, which define even as they obscure what we mean by justice. As Stuart Hall (1979) has observed, ideology is at its most powerful when it goes unnoticed, when it is taken for granted. John Cawleti (1976) argues that the formulaic dimension of the genre produces "stock plots" that frame our very imagination about crime and justice. Crime stories address the social issues of a particular time even as they reaffirm a society's dominant values, values that entail that society's sense of justice.

Some scholars who analyze the crime genre's ideologies focus on a unifying theme, for example, the relationship between crime and the political economy. Ernest Mandel (1984) takes a Marxian perspective and ties such matters as crime and even the significance of murder to shifts in the economy. Jon Thompson (1993) agrees that the genre reflects the structures of capitalism, but he also sees it as addressing the renewal and disintegration of empire. Christopher Breu (2005) discusses the relationship of crime to a post–World War II crisis of masculinity. There is an economic dimension to this crisis because that period witnessed a shift from craft and small business to the rise of the corporate form.

Of course, not all assessments that address ideology in the crime genre focus on economic dimensions. Sherlock Holmes, with his chemical experiments and cataloged knowledge of crime and criminals, represented scientific inquiry at a time when the scientific method was increasingly popular; science had applications for understanding and solving crime (Harrington 2007). Moreover, Doyle's choice of crimes was ideological in nature: despite rising corporate power and crime syndicates in London, Holmes primarily investigates small, individualistic crimes (Knight 2004). To the degree that Doyle depicts an organizational dimension to crime, it focuses on the archvillain Professor Moriarty, who "is the organizer of half that is evil and nearly all that is undetected in this great city" (1967, 303). Holmes also personified the virtues of his day, including loyalty to the monarchy. Ellen Harrington argues that Holmes effectively contains the threat of crime and the danger that it poses "by reinscribing the constancy and validity of familiar Victorian values at a time when such values were increasingly open to question and doubt" (2007, 372). She notes that the Holmes stories are an important reference point in portraying the detective as a sentinel on an outpost who guards society.

Other classic detectives also represent ideological positions. Agatha Christie's Miss Marple offered solutions to crimes that reflected the values of the small village (Knight 2004). Notwithstanding their critique of social institutions, Raymond Chandler's and Dashiell Hammett's detective stories ultimately reaffirmed dominant social values. In Chandler's *Murder My Sweet* (1944), for example, Philip Marlowe explains that he remains on a case despite pressure to drop it because he is like a small businessman trying to follow up on a sale. Similarly, in Hammett's *The Maltese Falcon* (1941), Sam Spade asserts his commitment to discovering who killed Miles Archer for reasons of loyalty; Spade did not like Archer and was even having an affair with Archer's wife, but Archer was Spade's partner. Both Spade and Marlowe embody the view of the detective as being on that outpost of a society in decay, but their resolution to cases overlays what Steven Knight calls "a conservative and fully bourgeois romantic structure" (1980, 152).

Ideologies change with the times. In his treatise on law and crime in US film and television, Timothy Lenz (2003) argues that the time period beginning in the 1950s and ending at the turn of the twenty-first century witnessed a significant shift in ideological positions. He describes the 1950 and 1960s as an era wherein the crime genre in film and on television took more of a liberal ideological position. Private detectives and defense lawyers were important characters. For example, heroic lawyers like Perry Mason produced justice by proving in court that their clients were innocent of the crimes with which they were wrongfully charged. Justice meant freeing the innocent. A generation of young people who were fans of such programs and the messages they conveyed became lawyers. There were, of course, police procedurals during the era that Lenz labels as predominantly "liberal," and some of these programs still exhibited a conservative law-and-order ideology. *Dragnet* returned to the air in the 1960s. Although this new version addressed some social issues and continued the documentary style of its 1950s version, it also carried a pronounced antiliberal ideology: the program criticized hippies and student dissidents and conveyed a stern antidrug message.

The 1970s was a transition period in which the crime genre shifted from a liberal to a more conservative ideology; this shift was largely completed by the 1980s (Lenz 2003). Other scholars (Brunsdon 2000; Cooke 2003) have noted that this shift was coterminus with the political ascendancy of President Ronald Reagan in the United States and Prime Minister Margaret Thatcher in the UK and with a resurgence of extreme political conservatism. From the 1980s through the 1990s a conservative ideology dominated television police procedurals. Programs like *Hill Street Blues* in the United States and *The Sweeney* in the UK presented a decaying social order with the police, sentinels on the urban outpost, being all that stood between society and chaos (also see Gitlin 1983).

Contemporary programs like *CSI* are less patently ideological, but they nonetheless reflect a conservative ideology. In contrast to *Perry Mason*, *CSI* portrays lawyers and sometimes even the law itself as impediments to a justice that is defined as capturing criminals. Moreover, because of their appeal to science, forensic procedurals have less of a need for law: science, not the law, produces justice (Cavender and Deutsch 2007). There is a focus on law and order in many contemporary procedurals. For example, on programs like *Law & Order* crime's threat to society is so great that order takes precedence over law, and these ends justify almost any means. To secure the social order, detectives may bend or even break the law, engaging in what Lenz (2003, 165) calls "testilying" in court, crossing the line with respect to rules about search and seizure or hitting suspects. In their construction, the story lines of these programs invite viewers to see such measures, albeit admittedly extreme, as necessary to restore order.

Even a recent television crime series like *Law & Order SVU* (1999–), which features women in lead roles and focuses on crimes of violence against women, traffics in conservative stereotypes. The program interrogates feminist themes about violence against women but often also contains implicit misogynistic messages (Cuklanz and Moorti 2006).

Despite the conservative ideological tendencies in the television crime genre over the past several decades, we are interested in locating programs or moments within programs that take a more progressive stance. We now turn to a discussion of the images of justice in *Prime Suspect* to examine its tendencies and contradictions vis-à-vis our model of progressive moral fiction.

Prime Suspect Justice

Although they praise the series, some scholars conclude that *Prime Suspect* is neither feminist nor progressive (Jermyn 2003; Tomc 1995; Thornham 1994). In part this is because the series adheres to the conventions of the crime genre and also because of the strictures of television. In this book, however, we have argued thus far that *Prime Suspect* constitutes a significant departure from other television police dramas. While legalistic in many respects, the series also conveys weaknesses in the law and in policing, problems that not only make it difficult to prosecute criminals but also importantly deny equal protection to poor children, transgender individuals, immigrants, and communities of color. Despite these social realist tendencies in the series, *Prime Suspect* also identifies fissures whereby Tennison uses the law and the police organization to offer hope to socially marginalized victims and to bring change to the police organization and, in so doing, to the crime genre. She and the series are by no means perfect on all dimensions, but they offer moments that transcend more limited notions of criminal justice.

Throughout the series, Jane Tennison exhibits a nuanced sense of justice but at the same time displays keen insights about the limitations on her ability to always accomplish justice. At times this sense of justice is very legalistic; that is, it is defined by knowledge of procedures and evidentiary requirements. In *Prime Suspect 1*, for example, Tennison knows that she cannot meet the legal evidentiary requirements for charging the prime suspect, Marlow. She believes Marlow to be guilty, but, in contrast to her predecessor, DCI Sheffard, she knows the limits of the law and releases Marlow. She then directs an investigation that uncovers the evidence needed to convict him. The episode reveals several justice themes that recur in later episodes: a sense of retribution but one that presumes equal protection; an opposition to those who behave as if they are above the law, whether they are police or community members; the willingness to innovate to achieve justice; and an expanded notion of the community that police serve.

In both dialogue and action Tennison exhibits a sense of justice and police duty to serve an increasingly diverse community. In *Prime Suspect 1* she makes clear that this community includes prostitutes despite numerous comments by her subordinates and other police personnel that devalue these women. Other officers refer to prostitutes as "tarts" or "slags" and either trivialize their victimization or blame them for it. In contrast, Tennison treats prostitutes with respect, a normalized interaction that also yields important breaks in the case that might not otherwise have occurred. Disdain for the devaluing of prostitutes by police is a recurrent theme in other works by *Prime Suspect* creator Lynda La Plante. For example, in La Plante's novel *Above Suspicion* DCI James Langton, who is heading an investigation into the serial murders of women who are mostly prostitutes, says, "They were all alive, once. . . . Now they're dead and whether or not they were junkies, whores, drunks, or just fucked-up human beings, they have a right to have us hunt down who killed them" (2001, 24).

The seven *Prime Suspect* episodes portray the wide diversity in the communities served by the police and the disparate notions held by individual police about those communities. In *Prime Suspect 2*, which deals with the murder of an African Caribbean woman, repeated racial slurs by a member of the investigative team, DI Frank Burkin, produced a sharp reprimand from Tennison and threats that he could be "sacked." Tennison also drives this point home to a subordinate who makes derogatory remarks about immigrants in *Prime Suspect 6: The Last Witness*. She tells him: "Look, I don't know what kind of ideas you have about the community we serve, but they'd better expand to include Jasmina." In *Prime Suspect 3* the police are investigating the death of a teenage male prostitute and a pedophile ring. This investigation generates a round of homophobic remarks from some of the police investigators, and in the course of interactions one highly respected male officer "comes out" to the team. In conversation he strongly criticizes the stereotypes being bandied about during team meetings, and Tennison supports him. These plots and scenes are consistent with Robert Reiner's (1994) argument that television police dramas sometimes reflect changes in police organization. They also are consistent with Ian Loader and Aogan Mulcahy's (2003) discussion of the increasing diversity of the police organization and growing recognition by the police of the diverse communities that they serve, a phenomenon the authors term "democratic cosmopolitanism."

Prime Suspect episodes also indicate Tennison's strong sense of retributive justice, although there are variations in what the idea means to her. Sometimes Tennison exhibits a classic philosophical sense of retribution: crime demands punishment (see Duff and Garland 1994). Along these lines, Tennison believes that it is her job to identify and apprehend the guilty so that they can be punished, or, as she puts it, "I think it is my job to catch the bad guys. Full stop" (*Prime Suspect 5: Errors in Judgment*). At other times she offers a more Durkheimian sense of retribution that entails restoring the equilibrium that crime has disrupted. In *Prime Suspect 4*: "Scent of Darkness," Tennison expresses this variant in terms of the victim's family, although, interestingly, she distinguishes it from justice in a larger sense: "Yeah, justice, of course, of course, I believe in justice, but retribution as well, it's very important. See, I had this case a couple of years ago. . . . There was this killer who walked free, suspended sentence. I mean, the guy definitely did it. Jesus, I get angry about it still. Well, how do you think the families of the victims feel? I mean, they need retribution; it helps them sleep at night. They've got to be able to believe in the system."

In its classic formulation, retributive justice presumes a sense of equal protection, of fairness (Murphy 1973). Tennison's expanded sense of the communities served by the police (discussed above) addresses this component of retribution. In dialogue throughout the series, she asserts that she wants law and order for everyone, and this does not seem to mean the conservative variant that is the goal in so many police procedurals. In *Prime Suspect 5: Errors in Judgment*, as Tennison attempts to solve the murder of a young drug dealer in a poor neighborhood, she and her superior disagree about the role of the police in poor communities. DCS Martin Ballinger (John McCardle) advocates a containment approach wherein the police cordon off low-income housing and try to keep the crime in these primarily minority communities from overflowing into white middle-class neighborhoods. Tennison responds: "Containment—that's the euphemism of the century. Ghettoization is more like it. . . . What about those poor sods who are born into the ghetto? What about them? You can't have one system of justice for the bad guys and one for everyone else. You can, but it's not a system that I want anything to do with." Her opposition to Ballinger's containment approach is grounded in a sense of fairness, of law and order for everyone.

Tennison's sense of justice includes disdain for those who act as if they are above the law. This obviously includes criminals but also those who engage in corrupt practices or in vigilantism. Police corruption is a frequent theme in the series, and it comes in many forms: detectives having sex with prostitutes who are their informants (*Prime Suspect 1*); a high-ranking police officer who participates in a pedophile ring (*Prime Suspect 3*); Tennison's superior, who secretly works with a drug kingpin not for bribes but rather as an accommodation to "contain" drug-related violence (*Prime Suspect 5: Errors in Judgment*). In each case, corruption breeds more corruption as individual officers or the police hierarchy try to cover up the corrupt behavior; for example, DS Otley conceals evidence by removing an incriminating page that contains DCI Sheffard's name from a prostitute's appointment book (*Prime Suspect 1*). Tennison's discovery of corruption in these episodes reinforces an important point in the social science literature about men officers' resistance to women officers: men officers fear that women officers who discover problematic behavior will not cover it up as readily as will the men (Hunt 1990). Indeed, Otley is livid that Tennison's discovery will taint Sheffard's record.

There are other, nonpolice examples of corruption in *Prime Suspect* as well. The pedophile ring in *Prime Suspect 3* includes, in addition to the high-ranking officer, a respected community leader. In *Prime Suspect 4:* "Inner Circles," Tennison discovers that several respectable citizens are part of a fraudulent real estate transaction. *Prime Suspect 7: The Final Act* focuses on an adult man, a teacher who is having sex with a teenage girl. These cases, like those that involve the police, breed further corruption, including a motive for murder.

Tennison's disdain for corruption can be linked to her commitment to law and order. She thinks that everyone, including the poor, the police, and community elites, should be equally bound by the same legal obligations. This view also explains her opposition to vigilantism. Her goal is to produce a system that offers equal protection from crime to rich and poor alike, and such a system would in turn legitimate both the police and the law. If people believe in the system, that is, that the state will apprehend and punish criminals, there will be no need for vigilante justice. An interesting discussion of the meaning of justice, including vigilante justice, occurs in *Prime Suspect 6: The Last Witness*, which deals with the victims of ethnic cleansing. Members of the Muslim community have kidnapped war criminal Dragon Yankovic and plan to return him to Bosnia because they doubt that the British government will try him for war crimes. Tennison learns that the Muslims have acted upon information supplied by her friend Robert West. In the following piece of dialogue, an irate Tennison confronts West on a bridge:

TENNISON: You fucked it up for me!

WEST: Kasim asked questions—intelligent, direct, honest questions. I wasn't going to lie to him. . . . He came to his own conclusions. He couldn't find justice in this country, and letting Zigic take the drop alone and protecting Yankovic is an insult to the two women he murdered.

TENNISON: How's this going to help them?

WEST: I met a few Yankovics in Bosnia, but I met a lot more Kasims, broken, stuck, no redress. The only way he was ever going to have any kind of peace, to have a life with some way forward, was to feel that justice had been done.

TENNISON: And what his friends are doing right now to Yankovic, you call that justice?

WEST: Yep. Kasim doesn't have murder in him.

TENNISON: And what about the other men? What you set into motion goes against everything I believe in, everything I stand for!

WEST: I know.

The two part company, leaving the bridge in different directions. Tennison mobilizes the police to find the kidnapped Yankovic.

We argue that part of Tennison's status as a justice provocateur involves her innovation in the face of barriers to doing justice. Although positive in many respects, her innovations also sometimes involve using ethically

Tennison argues with journalist and ex-lover Robert West about vigilante justice.

problematic tactics to achieve worthy ends. Several times we have referenced a pedophile ring that contained a high-ranking officer and a respected citizen in *Prime Suspect 3*. Tennison's dilemma is that as she tries to solve the murder of a young male prostitute, the police hierarchy and a community leader actively oppose her, and these are people with a lot of power. Tennison offers a compromise that the police hierarchy accepts: she will not pursue the high-ranking officer/pedophile if the hierarchy will cease its opposition to her efforts in the murder investigation. Tennison still has a problem in terms of the community leader. Despite her certainty of his guilt, there is not enough evidence to convict him. Tennison secretly gives the results of her investigation—results that implicate the community leader—to a journalist. In a rough sense, Tennison's innovation is retributive because the journalist's news story will destroy the community leader's reputation: he will "pay" for his crimes.

There is another roughly retributive innovation in *Prime Suspect 4*: "Inner Circles," an episode that deals with financial corruption among the members of an elite private club. A murderer has confessed, but Tennison thinks that he was goaded into the killing, and she suspects a local upper-class woman, Maria Henry (Jill Baker), who denies any involvement. Tennison interrogates Maria's daughter, Polly (Kelly Reilly), with Maria present, feigning a belief that Polly was the culprit. The interrogation is so harsh that Maria breaks down and confesses. Maria is diminished in Polly's eyes.

Tennison's most interesting innovations occur in *Prime Suspect 6: The Last Witness*. MI6 has invoked the Official Secrets Act to prevent Tennison from investigating Lukic/Yankovic's role in killing the Blekic sisters. As described in Chapter 3, Tennison cleverly deceives Lukic's wife into an admission that her husband is a government informant. Tennison secretly records the admission and plays the tape to another man. She rightly speculates that this man will be angered that Lukic/Yankovic is an informant. She is correct, and the man admits that he and Yankovic murdered the real Lukic. This innovation is more overtly retributive because Tennison can

Tennison travels to Bosnia to see the site where the Blekic sisters and others were tortured or killed.

then charge Yankovic with murder, a murder charge that is not included in MI6's promise of immunity to him.

Although Tennison's actions often produce justice, they are not unproblematic. In several episodes, for example, when she discovers corruption, the men's fears of her status as an outsider are well founded: she stops the corrupt behavior. At the same time, Tennison keeps the knowledge within the organization and trades her silence for organizational gains, including getting to remain on a case in several episodes. In *Prime Suspect 3*, the episode about the pedophile ring and the murder of a teenage prostitute, Tennison is twice warned to drop her murder investigation by superiors because of the involvement of a high-ranking police officer. Tennison bucks the hierarchy even as she offers a compromise: she will continue the case, but after she captures the murderer, she promises to discontinue the investigation and to protect the high-ranking officer from further prosecution. Tennison goes one step further in this compromise. Not only will she be permitted to continue the case, but the cost of her silence (i.e., protecting the organization from embarrassing revelations) is that her superiors must put her forward for a promotion.

Tennison opposes police corruption but sometimes practices organizational blackmail. She opposes vigilantism but engages in a form of vigilantism in *Prime Suspect 3* when she is unable to arrest the community leader and instead gives her case records to a journalist. Her intense interrogation of Polly in *Prime Suspect 4*: "Inner Circles," produces the desired result—her mother's confession—but it was, nonetheless, strategically and brutally harsh. When her assistant congratulates her, Tennison answers, "She [the mother] used her, and we did the same. What's the difference?" Similarly, Tennison's innovative actions in *Prime Suspect 6: The Last Witness*, netted a conviction against a murderer/war criminal by deceiving Lukic/Yankovic's wife. It can be argued that, on the one hand, Tennison's innovative actions make her a provocateur for justice because they bring justice for socially marginalized and often ignored victims. On the other hand, she engages in the sort of "order above law" behavior that we attributed to other, more conservative police dramas. Still, she does not engage in many of the tactics depicted and glorified in other police dramas, including tricking suspects into forgoing legal representation, condoning the beating of suspects, and conducting illegal searches. Even Tennison's ethically questionable actions are portrayed in such a manner as to make the audience uncomfortable with her conduct. These moments create the opportunity for discussions that weigh the balance of means and ends in the pursuit of justice.

Tennison's investigations produce insights for her (and the audience) about the lives of the socially marginalized at the heart of her investigations. Sometimes these are microlevel insights that humanize characters who are treated in a superficial, dismissive manner in other police dramas. Thus, in *Prime Suspect 1* Tennison learns that a murdered prostitute accepted one final (and deadly) customer because she needed the money for her child and that the other prostitutes took up a collection for her funeral. Tennison and the audience become aware of the plight of immigrants in *Prime Suspect 6: The Last Witness*: Jasmina Blekic, a medical student in Bosnia, now cleans toilets in a hospital, and her sister, Samira, worked twelve hours a day, then walked for an hour to get home because her earnings were not enough even for mass transit. At other times, *Prime Suspect* offers macrolevel insights: like many real immigrants, despite their victimization, the Blekic sisters were afraid to call the police for help. Tennison's growing awareness of these social problems fuels her motivation to deliver justice for socially marginalized victims.

In many episodes her insights about the experiences of these characters acknowledge the larger social context of their existence and their actions. The characters trapped in neighborhoods where drugs and crime rule, young people who are at the mercy of adults who abuse them, or the sexism, racism, and homophobia that are endemic in society (and in the police organization) constitute the social dimension of individual lives. In these situations Tennison looks for the fissures, for an edge that will allow her to innovatively circumnavigate the power of the police hierarchy or those with power and privilege in society and still accomplish her goal. The point of the series is that she tries. Indeed, her struggles—sometimes victories and sometimes defeats—are perhaps why *Prime Suspect* has been so popular.

In *Prime Suspect 5: Errors in Judgment* her supervisor, DCS Ballinger, tells Tennison that she is a role model, an icon on the police force. Interestingly, scholars and critics have called Tennison an iconic character, a hero for our time (Creeber 2001). Tennison tries to do justice, in the words of her dad in *Prime Suspect 6: the Last Witness*, "do what's right." Even so, Tennison's actions that try to secure justice for marginalized victims or to challenge an unjust hierarchy are usually hers alone. As an individual she makes a difference, but her behavior never involves much sense of collective action. Perhaps, as several scholars have noted, the idea of the individualist, a lone sentinel on the outpost, is a crime genre tradition that is hard to overcome. On a brighter note, the real-life upper-echelon British women police administrators suggested that they were able to work with other women and men to implement organizational policies that improved conditions for those who came after them.

Conclusion

There are ideological dimensions to the crime genre. Both historically and today, notwithstanding some exceptions, there is a conservative slant to the genre, especially in terms of its messages about the meaning of justice, of law and order. Criminals signify a threat to the social order and must be apprehended and punished. Although *Prime Suspect* adheres to some of this tradition (Tennison catches criminals and even expressly advocates retribution), the series also conveys a sense that retributive justice is not guaranteed by the criminal justice system. Members of elite social classes or upper-echelon police officers are often able to victimize members of socially disadvantaged groups without being called to account. Tennison's insistence on extending equal protection to those members of the lower social strata often results in organizational impediments and outright threats to her career. Yet she perseveres and develops innovative ways of acquiring justice for the socially marginalized.

Although Tennison is not a self-professed feminist, she and the series fit within the label of the feminist crime genre; for example, she exhibits a relentless obligation to seek justice for victims who otherwise have few expectations of such help, especially from the police. Moreover, the series exemplifies elements of a progressive moral fiction: Tennison and the audience glean insights from characters' experiences, which are often grounded in a larger social context. Despite an array of powerful forces that are aligned against these characters (and against Tennison), including gendered organizations, anti-immigrant sentiments, and governmental apathy, she is always on the alert to beat impediments and produce justice. In these moments Tennison exhibits the characteristics of what we have described as a provocateur for justice (Aiken 2001). She exemplifies the possibility of obtaining justice for socially marginalized victims and demonstrates that even a large impersonal bureaucratic organization like the police can be maneuvered to treat such individuals respectfully.

Through dialogue and story line, the series directly addresses justice issues that surround policing and raises questions about contemporary social issues. There are discussions and debates between Tennison and other characters as to what constitutes justice and the proper role of police in promoting it. We argue that the series addresses these issues in a progressive way; for example, story lines detail how people's lives are negatively affected by social inequality and ensuing relations of oppression and domination (see Young 1990). Yet Tennison is not a social revolutionary figure. She can be falsely empathetic and deceitful, and she embraces the role of police officer catching bad guys. And this role restricts the level of change that she can bring to a society filled with injustices: it restricts the extent of social transformation that is shown in the *Prime Suspect* series. She acts in concert with others, directing her team toward the accomplishment of these ends, but for the most part she is isolated and sustains no larger-scale collective actions to promote social or organizational change. But it is a beginning.

These very limitations make Tennison a believable and compelling character. Also, the open-ended nature of some episodes—an arrest may not produce justice or even closure—makes *Prime Suspect* a useful pedagogical device. The series can focus discussions around key individual and social issues: how individuals who work in large or even problematic organizations might advance in their careers and still do the right thing; the communities that the police serve; the hope for justice in societies with brutally unjust social arrangements. Unlike many other television police dramas, *Prime Suspect* generates as many questions about justice as it answers.

As we have noted, *Prime Suspect* resembles earlier social realism productions that addressed social problems issues. These productions locate individual problems within their social context. We now turn to a discussion of the social problems dimension of the series.

CHAPTER 5

Private Troubles and Public Issues

The crime genre has long been characterized by individualism; that is, the criminal bears individual responsibility for his or her crime, and the investigator, a strong and heroic individual, apprehends the culprit. The depiction of the criminal as an evil villain and the detective/cop as the strong hero who saves the day is at the heart of the crime genre's individualistic narrative, a narrative that privileges a binary of good and evil. Restoring order or status quo arrangements has also been a common theme in the genre. Indeed, as the name of one of television's most popular crime genre programs suggests, the point is "law and order," not some progressive agenda. The plots and development of crime genre characters are rarely progressive, and many crime genre programs traffic in unidimensional gender, racial, sexual, class, and national stereotypes. Notable exceptions to these generalities exist, and some will be referenced later, but multidimensional and varied portraits of women, people of color, and gay/lesbian/transgender and other socially marginalized characters are underrepresented in television generally and in the crime genre in particular. Social problems are often vastly oversimplified and are portrayed either as irresolvable or as easily remedied by simple acts of individual goodwill.

As we have noted, our model of progressive moral fiction implies works that offer realistic and sensitive insights into the experiences of socially marginalized groups and locates those experiences within a larger societal context. In this chapter we consider the extent to which the *Prime Suspect* series provides such insights and a social location for its characters. Our analysis includes an examination of the complexities and nuances of portrayals of crime, criminals, and law. We will argue that the series transcends simplistic and individualized notions of crime causation. Yet *Prime Suspect's* treatment in this regard is not completely new or isolated in television or the crime genre. In Chapter 1 we discussed how the feminist crime genre works to address the social context of crime as it decenters the heterosexual male domination of the genre. Similarly, work by authors such as African American writer Walter Mosley has challenged negative racial stereotypes in the crime genre. Still earlier social problems films of the 1930s, 1940s, and 1950s addressed a variety of social issues, and British social realism television, which had its heyday in the late 1950s and early 1960s, offered coverage of social issues and working-class communities in a realistic, semi-documentary, although often melodramatic format (Cooke 2003).

We will briefly address the history of social problems and social realism film and television and then note the departure from such formats in British television of the 1970s onward as well as the general avoidance of social issue programming in US television throughout the years. We then move on to an analysis of *Prime Suspect's* treatment of social issues, in particular, how moments within episodes offer insights into the experiences of socially marginalized persons. Although the series often disrupts the binary between good and evil and destabilizes the white male dominance of the genre, it does not offer comprehensive, modernist policy solutions to social problems.

Social Problems, Social Realism, and the Crime Genre

The crime genre tends to locate crime at an individual level, using and constantly reproducing a binary of good and evil, of heroes and villains. The crime genre also conveys a sense of alienation and social malaise and even deals with the meaning of order and threats to that order (Krutnik 1991; Brunsdon 2000; Mizejewski 2004). Despite its individualistic focus, sometimes the crime genre also addresses social issues.

In the post–World War II period, a number of film genres addressed social problems themes. Some films during this period employed cinematic techniques to enhance their sense of realism while also demonstrating a consciousness of social issues, including alcoholism (*The Lost Weekend*, 1945) and anti-Semitism (*Crossfire*, 1947). One film, *The Best Years of Our Lives* (1946), followed the lives of three veterans who have adjustment problems after they return from World War II. The men deal with war injuries, unemployment, marital breakup, and drinking problems as they try to readjust to civilian life.

Some crime genre films during this period also used the social problems theme as a narrative overlay onto the more standard crime story line. *The Blue Dahlia* (1946) parallels *The Best Years of Our Lives* in that it also follows three returning war veterans. Two of these are secondary characters who confront economic difficulties such as finding and affording a place to live; they have to room together. One of these men, Buzz Wanchek (William Bendix), experiences uncontrollable bursts of anger and blackouts as a result of a war injury to his head. The third veteran, the film's protagonist, Johnny Morrison (Alan Ladd), discovers that his wife has been unfaithful while he was away and has even caused the death of their son. He, too, has problems controlling his temper and is wrongly suspected of murdering his wife. All three men realize that while they were at war, others who stayed behind have prospered and enjoyed "the good life" (Luhr 1991).

Individual criminality was deemphasized in some of these crime films in favor of a more sociological perspective. Social problems thrillers employed documentary-like techniques to varying degrees, but they also utilized many familiar conventions of the crime narrative. Such films came to dominate the cinematic crime genre during the 1950s, although it was also during the 1950s that television overtook film and radio as the most popular entertainment form.

A commitment to social realism characterized much television in the UK beginning in the late 1950s. These programs sought to convey a sense of working-class communities and often highlighted social problems with an aim to provide insights into social interventions that could promote public welfare, for example, *Emergency-Ward 10* (1951–67). This form of programming offered hope that societal ills could be solved through enlightened policy intervention. Police series in this era included *Fabian of Scotland Yard* (1954–56) and *Dixon of Dock Green* (1955–76), series that offered a sense of realism as well as the reassurance of effective and fair police protection of the community. The 1960s have been described as a golden age for such UK programming (Cooke 2003). Social realism television was never as prominent in the United States because of the more commercial nature of its television industry. A notable exception was the series *Eastside Westside* (1963–64), which dealt with a New York City social worker and addressed a number of controversial issues relevant to American inner cities. The series had immediate difficulty gaining sponsors.

Like British television, popular US police television programs in the 1950s and 1960s generally provided a sense that police were trustworthy protectors; some series (e.g., *Dragnet* and *The Untouchables*) evoked a televisual sense of realism. Also in the 1960s, the highly successful UK police drama *Z Cars* (1962–78) began to aim for even more realism than its television predecessors and to portray violence and police wrongdoing as more routine dimensions of police life.

By the 1970s social unrest, the visibility of state coercion, and the election of conservative governments were associated with more escapist television, on the one hand, and programs that showed the violent nature of policing, on the other (e.g., *The Sweeney*). The dominance of social realism programs began to waiver in the UK as people began to question the viability of modernist policy proscriptives for social ills (Cooke 2003). The economics of Thatcherism also demanded that UK television become more competitive and commercially viable, akin to the US television industry (also see Jermyn 2010). UK and US police programs in the 1970s and 1980s increasingly aimed for a sense of cinematic realism coupled with an action and adventure crime-fighting format. These programs conveyed a sense of almost constant danger on urban streets, and in such an apparently dangerous milieu, the occasional violence and corruption among police seemed an almost necessary evil.

The popular 1980s US series *Hill Street Blues* (1981–87) exemplifies how social realism and police drama increasingly included a sense of urban chaos, danger, and occasional police excess. Although the program frequently addressed the social roots of urban violence and criminality, it did so in a way that questioned traditional liberal solutions to social problems. Urban poverty was a constant backdrop to these stories, but the series tended to present the poor, who were frequently persons of color, in stereotypic, underclass roles. Several scholars have argued that overall the program conveyed a message that the police—even if flawed— were a crucial buffer protecting middle-class society from a chaotic and dangerous urban world (Gitlin 1983; Curti 1988). Jane Rhodes challenges the "realism" claims of *Hill Street Blues* because it routinely denied black women ongoing or fully developed characters: "Black women formed the backdrop of poverty, crime and hopelessness upon which the plots were built. They were hookers and drug addicts, abused wives and rape victims, but rarely cops or public defenders or upstanding members of the community" (1991, 427). Moreover, although white women were featured in lead roles and there were moments when women's issues were examined, the program predominantly focused on the perspectives and experiences of police *men* (Curti 1988). Gitlin (1983) refers to *Hills Street Blues* as the first postliberal cop show.

Of course, not every television police drama made the shift to a more conservative perspective. In the Introduction we discussed several police dramas from the 1980s that featured women in lead roles. Not only did *The Gentle Touch* and *Juliet Bravo* in the UK and *Cagney & Lacey* in the United States deal with the difficulties that women face in the traditionally male-dominated field of policing, they also addressed a variety of social issues that were relevant to women regardless of occupation. In one *Juliet Bravo* episode, for example, Inspector Jean Darblay must deal with an armed man who has been abusive to his wife and is holding their daughter hostage. The man has become unstable because he lost his job when the local mill closed, a common occurrence in the British economy during the time when the series was made.

By the 1990s a number of highly popular police dramas dominated prime-time programming along with reality crime television programs. These programs addressed contemporary social problems but typically from a very conservative perspective that stressed the evil nature of criminals and the hopelessness of progressive policies and legal structures. In *NYPD Blue* (1993–2005), for example, citizens and the police alike are shown to be overwhelmed by social forces such as homelessness, single motherhood, and teenage sexuality. The program seems to suggest that, given the impossibility of the situation, it is no surprise that officers sometimes "lose it" and slap or even beat suspects. Because these are continuing characters, we know them and come to share their sense of frustration.

A number of scholars stress that the crime genre is frequently a vehicle for addressing relevant social concerns from a variety of perspectives, including more progressive approaches (Brunsdon 2000; Mizejewski 2004). The feminist crime genre offers myriad examples of efforts to decenter the male-dominated genre and open up broader visions of social justice for socially marginalized persons and groups. An increasing number of crime genre novels treat racism as a social problem and offer multidimensional portraits of chief protagonists and other characters of color.

Walter Mosley's Easy Rollins details the violence, emotional harm, and injustices associated with racism in the larger society. In one of his novels, Mosley essentially rewrites a racist scene from a classic crime novel. In Raymond Chandler's novel *Farewell My Lovely* (1940) the white male hero goes to an all-black music club early in the story. The club and the black people in it are described by Chandler from the white detective's perspective in a stereotypic and derogatory manner. This scene inspired Mosley's narrative in his now-classic crime novel *Devil in a Blue Dress* (1990). In an early passage, Mosley describes a bar and a white villain's menacing visit to it. Mosley's rewrite changes the audience's perspective to that of a black protagonist. This scene also appears in the excellent film adaptation of Mosley's book (1995) starring Denzel Washington.

Mosley's treatment gets beyond racial stereotypes but continues to reify many gender stereotypes, often through the sexualization of female characters. Barbara Neely's Blanche White novel series (*Blanche on the Lam* [1992], *Blanche among the Talented Tenth* [1994], *Blanche Cleans Up* [1998], *Blanche Passes Go* [2001]) examines the convergence of gender, race, and class issues in the life of her African American domestic worker protagonist. Neely turns characters that are often treated in a stereotypic or almost invisible manner in much other crime fiction into the central protagonists, who see and know all simply because much of white society fails to even notice that they are present. The *Prime Suspect* series uses similar techniques to both satirize and decenter the white male–dominated television police procedural.

Prime Suspect and Social Issues

We argue that *Prime Suspect* goes further than the women-centered police television series of the 1980s to weave social dimensions more deeply into the central crime plot story line. We also suggest that, relative to most police procedurals, this series offers more complex and sensitive portraits of socially marginalized individuals and contemporary social issues both within and outside of the police organization.

Instead of a simple twin plot format as in *Cagney & Lacey*, social dimensions are at the core of the *Prime Suspect* series crime plots. Perhaps this was an extension of the logic of those 1980s police dramas; perhaps it was a conscious decision to be more edgy, to do something new, something that might attract an audience. In this the *Prime Suspect* series had the advantage of not being a weekly series with the demands on the writers and actors that sometimes diminish a program's intensity and force productions back to tired conventions. The extended format of the series allowed for superior character development and plot nuances. *Prime Suspect* has featured thorough research, strong writing, and great acting, which gave an intensity and contemporary feel to the crime story and which more carefully connected that story to a larger context.

Many *Prime Suspect* episodes foreground gender, race, and class inequalities as well as issues surrounding sexual orientation. The series depicts the barriers that these inequities impose on people and what happens when their lives are also touched by crime. For example, some episodes center on issues of racism or anti-immigrant sentiments and how these prejudices generate fragile relationships between the police and communities of color. Other episodes consider the outcomes that follow the sexual abuse and mistreatment of young people. Regardless of the issues involved, one of the strengths of the series is its treatment of the police as a social institution that contributes to rather than simply presides over these problematic social issues. We present an analysis of several *Prime Suspect* episodes to demonstrate how the series links social problems areas and crime.

The Gendered Police Organization: *Prime Suspect 1*

Prime Suspect 1 presents two parallel but integrated stories: Will the police discover the serial killer who murders women? Will DCI Tennison be allowed to do her job and earn the respect of superiors and subordinates? These parallel stories are grounded in a deeper treatment of a police organization, indeed of a society, that devalues women. In an early vivid scene, as the detectives race away to arrest their prime suspect, they take no notice as they pass the hearse that contains the woman victim's body, incorrectly presumed to be a prostitute. The male detectives also belittle the other prostitutes who had information relevant to the case.

Perhaps even more important is the script's treatment of George Marlow, the prime suspect. He seems to be a normal guy—in the words of one witness, "a bit of a lad." This characterization interestingly parallels the term for Tennison's team of detectives: "the lads." The lads indicate that Marlow seems like a "nice bloke" to them. *Prime Suspect 1* does not replay standard crime genre conventions of abusive males as visible outliers (Carmody 1998; Cuklanz and Moorti 2006). By including scenes of Marlow averring his innocence to his wife and of him acting as a dutiful son with his ailing mother, *Prime Suspect 1* challenges the standard assumption that aberrant strangers pose the greatest danger to women (see Dobash and Dobash 1979; Stanko 1985; Messerschmidt 2000). Marlow was known to his women victims because they were customers of his wife; they all trusted him to some extent. Until she was confronted with photographs of one of his victims, his wife viewed Marlow's sexual behavior toward her as a bit deviant but not really that far out of the norm.

Although the character of Marlow exaggerates the danger to women from serial killers, his demeanor as a normal and even likable fellow comports well with characterizations of men's violence against women as an extreme extension of men's patriarchal dominance over women (Stanko 1985). DCI Tennison must capture a serial killer and confront a sexist police organization, but the driving premise of *Prime Suspect 1* depends on the social fact of the devaluation of women in society—working women (including sex workers and policewomen), women witnesses, and women victims.

Visuals and dialogue convey at several points in the episode that police devalue sex workers but do have sex with them. Yet in the case of the death of a prostitute, the men fail to seriously consult with other prostitutes who might have knowledge of the crime. As a result, DCI Sheffard and his lads fail to make crucial headway on the case. Their hectic search for clues includes scenes of squealing tires and a frantic, action-packed pace. When juxtaposed with their ultimate failure to build an effective case against the prime suspect, these scenes can be viewed as a satirical send-up of earlier action-oriented, male-dominated procedurals like *The Sweeney* (Sydney-Smith 2009). Tennison takes over and leads the team to a successful outcome; she listens to the prostitutes, pays heed to subtle clues, and builds the case that Marlow is indeed a serial killer despite his "nice bloke" demeanor. Her successful resolution of the case and establishment of herself as head of a homicide investigation team decenters the male domination of the procedural subgenre.

Racism and Police: *Prime Suspect 2*

Prime Suspect 2 is centered on issues of racism both as individual prejudice and as embedded within the social structures of police organization and police/community relations. DCI Tennison heads an investigation into the murder of a young African Caribbean woman. Tennison must tread carefully in the investigation because of tense relations between the police and the African Caribbean community. She quickly encounters racism in the police organization, first from her peer, DCI Thorndike, who warns her not to trust the African Caribbean community, and second from a subordinate, DI Frank Burkin, who is so racist that he cannot be an effec-

Angry residents of an African Caribbean community confront Tennison and police at a neighborhood meeting.

tive detective. Burkin tells Tennison that he views the murdered woman as "one less of them on the street." She asks Burkin if skin color matters after you've been murdered.

Tennison threatens to fire Burkin but exhibits her own racial problematic. DS Bob Oswalde, a black man with whom she had a tryst at a conference, is assigned to her team. Tennison fears the consequences of a discovery of their relationship and tries to have Oswalde removed. When that fails, she treats him in an unprofessional manner, relegating him to menial chores, assignments that ironically parallel her treatment by her white male superiors in *Prime Suspect 1*.

Several scholars note that television typically neglects members of racial and ethnic minority populations or treats them in a negative, one-dimensional manner (Rhodes 1991; Gray 1995). Television news disproportionately features crime committed by people of color and portrays such populations in a violent and threatening manner (Chiricos and Eschholz 2002; Eschholz, Chiricos, and Gertz 2003). Such repetitive images, especially when they are so frequently repeated in reality television crime programs and police dramas, reinforce negative stereotypes about racial and ethnic minorities. In turn, these portraits generate support for punitive crime policies (Oliver and Armstrong 1998; Gilliam and Iyengar 2000). As one scholar notes, it is easy to support the "rule of police" (rather than the rule of law) when the police are policing "the other" (Grant 1992).

In her analysis of *Prime Suspect 2*, Brooks (1994) notes that the crime genre typically relies on stereotypes and mythology about blacks. Thus, in the opening scene of the episode, Tennison appears to be interviewing a black man who is a rape suspect. It turns out that the man is DS Oswalde and that this is a police conference role-play workshop on interviewing suspects. Even so, Oswalde offers a stereotypical set of statements that are often attributed to black male rapists (e.g., Brownmiller 1975; for critique, see Davis 1981). Within the scene there are also sexual undertones to the workshop interaction between Tennison and Oswalde that seem especially problematic when in the next scene we see that they are lovers. Yet when Tennison alludes in jest to the comments that Oswalde made in the training session about women liking it rough, Oswalde is offended that she might even jokingly associate such beliefs with him. He responds: "Hey, that wasn't me; I don't think that way."

Although problematic in its articulation of racial stereotypes, the opening scene offers the audience an opportunity to confront its own racial stereotypes, a point also noted by Jermyn (2010). Did the audience know that he was not a rapist, that this was a faux interrogation? If the audience accepted it as a real interrogation, did the audience find the scene offensive and stereotypical? This approach is still arguably a problematic and titillating display of racist stereotypes. Such stereotypes are even less thoughtfully included as dialogue in other contemporary police procedurals. One *Murder Investigation Team* episode features a black pimp who offers a "women like it rough" defense for his violence against women.

With respect to the crime genre, Reddy (2003) notes that many works go to great lengths to demonstrate that their white detectives are not racist. Often racism is presented as a personal prejudice that is unrelated to organization and power relations. Also, white detectives rarely question their own white privilege (Reddy 2003, 130, 166).

However, in *Prime Suspect 2* the audience witnesses Tennison's inappropriate treatment of Oswalde once he is assigned to her team. Her treatment of Oswalde may be a mere strategy for organizational survival; that is, she knows that her behavior is constantly under scrutiny by subordinates and superiors and that a sexual relationship with a subordinate, particularly someone on her investigative team, could jeopardize her career. Even so, Tennison's objection to Oswalde's assignment is stated in racialized terms: "It smacks of tokenism." Interestingly, although DCS Kernan initially praises Oswalde's outstanding record of service, he ultimately admits that he assigned Oswalde to the racially tense case because it would be good to have a "black face on the team." Kernan's explanation is consistent with an "additive" view of racial and ethnic officers in policing noted by police scholars (Brown and Heidensohn 2000). In part, Tennison is annoyed that Kernan appointed a new member to the team without consulting her. She resents Kernan's "token" approach, but her behavior still reinforces the institutionalized racism that is rampant in her police organization.

In another *Prime Suspect 2* scene, Oswalde visits Tennison's home to report on the results of his investigation and reason with her about how she is treating him. Oswalde discusses what he has discovered, and Tennison listens, amused. The following dialogue reflects the many parallels between the performance pressures that they both face as tokens in the police organization:

TENNISON: What are you trying to prove? It's as if you're trying to take some test all the time.

OSWALDE: Well, you are no different. . . . I watched you on the course. You know they're all lined up waiting to see you fall flat on your face. So you want to be the best . . . come out on top. Well, I'm the same as you.

After this interaction Tennison more fully incorporates Oswalde as an important member of the team. It is clear that both Tennison and Oswalde are driven to succeed in the police hierarchy despite its extreme racist and sexist character. This desire for career success leads both of them to at times replicate elements of sexism, racism, and authoritarianism that are integral to this hierarchy. Tennison's fear of discovery with regard to her affair leads her to replicate institutional racism in her treatment of Oswalde. Oswalde's drive to success leads him to conduct a harsh interrogation that results in the suicide of an innocent young black man.

Prime Suspect 2 tackles the problem of racism head-on. The episode demonstrates the effects of racism that are both internal and external to

Sergeant Oswalde prepares dinner at Tennison's flat while they discuss performance pressure in their jobs.

policing. *Prime Suspect 2* goes beyond individual racism to address institutionalized racism. We see Jane Tennison rebuking a racist officer but then engaging in actions that perpetuate racism in the organization by limiting DS Oswalde to menial work assignments. Oswalde's harsh interrogation of a young black male witness also illustrates the point made by critical race feminist Patricia Hill Collins (2000) that members of oppressed social groups can still act in ways that oppress others. Both Tennison and Oswalde so strongly aspire to success in policing that they often fail to challenge oppressive organizational norms. The episode can stimulate thought-provoking discussions of the ways in which race is embedded within organizations and institutions. Tennison's behavior in *Prime Suspect 2* reveals that even an individual ostensibly opposed to racism can reinforce such organizational disadvantage.

Policing Social Class:
Prime Suspect 4, "Inner Circles"

Prime Suspect 4, "Inner Circles," juxtaposes the lives of the wealthy elite with those who live in an impoverished housing estate. The wealthy enjoy comfortable lives as well as insider connections with the police. When a wealthy officer of a private club is murdered, Tennison's investigation leads her to question the club's manager as well as the victim's business associates. Nervous that Tennison's inquiry will uncover some shady real estate deals on the part of the victim and club members, the manager complains to police brass, who try to steer Tennison away from town elites and toward a young suspect, a known troublemaker who lives in the housing estates.

Tennison refuses to be warned off and perseveres in her investigation, aided by Detective Sergeant (DS) Chris Cromwell (Sophie Stanton), who is herself from a poor background. Cromwell's social class background provides an interesting contrast with Tennison's more middle-class language and demeanor. The investigation is complicated by Cromwell's history of resentment against the elite inner circle that she believes has always escaped accountability for wrongdoing in her community. A particularly tense scene shows angry citizens at a town council meeting. The council is approving the shady land development deal that most citizens strongly oppose. But the fix is on, and the council appears ready to approve the deal. Tennison and Cromwell are present in the audience, hoping to observe

DS Cromwell and Tennison are nearly arrested when a community hearing turns volatile.

the hearing process, which they believe is related to their investigation. When vocal community opposition escalates, the council orders the police to clear the hearing room. Police-citizen scuffles ensue, and Tennison and Cromwell, both in plain clothes, are manhandled by police. Cromwell resists and attempts to show the officer her ID. Community leaders use the incident to question Tennison's competence. Cromwell is about to be disciplined, and Tennison is almost removed from the case entirely. Tennison uses her accumulated evidence to pressure her superiors into allowing her and Cromwell to remain on the case. Tennison and Cromwell ultimately determine that the crimes were orchestrated by a woman who is a member of the community elite. Tennison extracts a confession from her, but it cannot be used in court to convict her.

The contrast of the privilege of community elites with the lives of residents in poor housing estates is a recurrent theme in the *Prime Suspect* series. While holding the poor accountable for criminal wrongdoing, Tennison nevertheless pursues justice in the cases of elite wrongdoing. True to patterns in the real world, the privileged often escape legal system sanctions. *Prime Suspect* does not always offer a happy ending in this regard.

However, it does suggest the complexities of holding more wealthy and connected persons responsible for criminal actions and ways in which class inequality figures into the criminal justice system.

Policing Immigration and Government Corruption: *Prime Suspect 6: The Last Witness*

Prime Suspect 6: The Last Witness confronts issues of immigration, nationalism, and the victimization of women that often accompanies these movements. The problems addressed in the episode, particularly the plight of immigrants—their fears and the invisibility and degradation associated with the work that they do as well as the torture and rape inflicted on the bodies and minds of women in the name of nationalist struggles—are rarely addressed in popular film and television or, for that matter, by international tribunals (Human Rights Watch 2001). Immigrants and war victims are often "ghosts" in our world—persons who are seen but unseen because they do much of the essential and basic labor in society but must remain hidden from officials' views and records and from our consciousness (Adelman, Cavender, and Jurik 2009). Avery Gordon (1997) employs the concept of ghosts, arguing that they serve as symptoms of phenomena missing from social reality and occasionally haunting our world. Attending to them can challenge taken-for-granted realities and lead to a transformative recognition that makes us understand both an oppressed past and future possibilities.

Prime Suspect 6: The Last Witness focuses our attention onto the hidden lives of immigrants and the hidden victimization of women in the atrocities of war (see Adelman, Cavender, and Jurik, 2009). In the story, Samira and Jasmina Blekic are sisters who immigrated to London after the Serbo-Croatian Wars (1991–95). They were victims of wartime torture and rape by a sadistic Serbian war criminal. Eleven years later, Samira is found tortured and murdered. Tennison heads the investigation, and her inquiries carry us into the world of immigrants working in London in low-paying, menial, "invisible labor" types of jobs. Tennison learns from their coworkers that the Blekic sisters wanted to be invisible because of their earlier victimization. Moreover, the atrocity in which Samira and Jasmina were victimized is not even recognized by international commissions as having occurred. Tennison travels to Bosnia to discover the truth about the events of years ago in order to unravel the mystery. She identifies the killer, a seemingly respectable London optician who is protected by the British government because he informs on other Serbian war criminals. Despite warnings from her superiors and at some risk to her career, Tennison finds a way to apprehend him for yet a third murder.

Prime Suspect 6: The Last Witness uses settings and visuals to simultaneously convey the hidden and socially marginal status of the Blekic sisters and Tennison's growing awareness of and connection with them as her investigation proceeds. Many scenes depict the sisters' (and indeed other immigrants') hidden status by showing them in what are literally underground settings. In the opening scene, Samira's body is discovered by immigrant day laborers in a basement at a construction site. The lighting in the basement scene and the accompanying soundtrack convey a sense of the place as eerie and terrible. The immigrant workers immediately flee the site, anxious that they will be discovered when the police arrive. A subsequent underground scene depicts Tennison and her detectives as they are led through the basement of a large luxury hotel where Samira had worked. Their guide, a hotel manager, is quickly lost in the basement labyrinth of his own hotel. There is a hub of activity in this underworld by the housekeeping staff, largely immigrants and people of color whom even the manager never sees. Workers direct the manager and detectives to Stephen Abacha (Femi Oguns), a coworker of Samira who is cleaning urinals. This scene offers a glimpse of the dungeonlike setting in which Samira and the other staff worked long hours for low wages to provide the luxury experienced by the wealthy guests. Abacha tells Tennison that Samira was Bosnian and that even though she could have had a better job, she preferred to work at the hotel so that she could remain invisible. Tennison asks him if the hotel will have an address for Samira, and he says, "Yes, but it will be false. They are like ghosts."

Another underground setting dominates the next scene: Tennison finds Samira's sister, Jasmina, hiding in an under-the-floor compartment in the apartment that the sisters had shared. Jasmina tells Tennison that Samira prepared the underground space because "she was making herself safe." Despite her sister's murder, Jasmina had not come forward because she feared the police and was afraid of being deported. Over the course of several interviews, Tennison learns the story of the Blekic sisters' victimization in Bosnia. Jasmina is also afraid because of Samira's murder, and Tennison promises to protect her. Later, Tennison and her detectives race through another underground world, this time in the basement of the hospital where Jasmina works. Tennison also is lost in the labyrinth and arrives too late: Jasmina has been shot dead. Ironically, Jasmina, a medical student in Bosnia, dies cleaning a hospital commode. The settings and visuals in *Prime Suspect 6: The Last Witness* make visible the often invisible experiences of immigrants and refugees from wartime atrocities, particularly women.

Prime Suspect 6: The Last Witness also reveals another social dimension that accompanies immigration debates today: the strong resentment and vilification of immigrants. In one scene, a politician on television rails against immigrants. He uses Samira's death to condemn "illegal immigrants," lamenting that London has been "swamped by foreign criminals." He lumps all immigrants into one problematic group. Other characters have little use for immigrants either. When the detectives question the foreman at the construction site where Samira's body was found (they want to interview the workers who found her), he can offer little information.

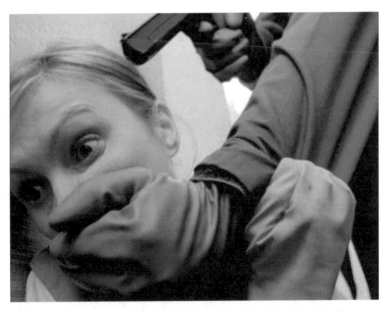

Jasmina Blekic is murdered while she cleans toilets at the hospital where she works.

He says about the workers, "I don't know them, don't mix with them. They just work for me, they're just casual workers." Some of the detectives on Tennison's team share this antipathy toward immigrants. The detectives are annoyed that it is so difficult to track down victims and witnesses. They purposely mispronounce immigrants' names, a tactic that reflects a deeper disrespect of people like Samira. Even MI6, the Secret Intelligence Service, although not overtly anti-immigrant, is aligned against refugees like Samira and Jasmina. An MI6 agent tells Tennison that since they have no record of the atrocity that Jasmina has described, it does not exist.

Not only does *Prime Suspect 6: The Last Witness* reveal the invisible, often underground worlds of the immigrants and the disdain that some citizens have for this community, but the episode gives this community a voice to reveal its feelings about the negative treatment that they experience. In one scene, after she has emerged from the underground compartment, Jasmina angrily responds to insulting stories in the newspaper. Jasmina tells Tennison: "No, she was not a prostitute. . . . She was honest and she was hard-working. We lost our parents and our house, and we came here because we thought it would be safe. And in ten years she has not taken a penny from you. I know how you despise us, how you think we are less than you because we do the filthy jobs, but we're not!" When Jasmina says "you," it is clear that she does not mean only Tennison but rather the entire nonimmigrant, native-born British community.

Prime Suspect 6: The Last Witness is an excellent episode for generating a classroom discussion about a very important contemporary social issue: immigration. Invisible in life, these murdered young women are like ghosts who haunt Tennison and cause her to see their lives, the horrible atrocities that motivated their immigration, and their negative experiences as immigrants in London. Their haunting moves Tennison to see other "invisibles," for example, a charwoman who cleans the hall in her dad's nursing home. The episode brings into sharp relief the resentment and stereotypes that confront immigrant people everywhere. It also demonstrates the special vulnerability of immigrants who can never call the police: they fear them. But to a degree, the episode gives immigrants like Jasmina Blekic a voice with which to defend themselves.

Table 5.1 provides an overview of the social issues and social groups that are addressed in the seven episodes of *Prime Suspect*.

Table 5.1. *Prime Suspect*'s Coverage of Socially Marginalized Groups
and the Structural Roots of Social Problems

Prime Suspect Episode	Socially Marginalized Groups	Structural Roots of Individual Problems
Prime Suspect 1	Prostitutes: disrespected; forced to have sex with police; their victimization not a police priority Women police officers: disrespected; passed over for meaningful assignments; sexualized; citizens prefer male police officers; work/life balance	Male-dominated police organization Corruption among male police buddies Patriarchal culture of disrespect and violence against women normalized Societal expectations about women's domestic work
Prime Suspect 2	African Caribbean community: disrespected; police brutality and failure to protect African Caribbean police sergeant: disrespected; passed over; given menial work assignments	Police mistreatment, disrespect, and ignorance about the community Overt and institutionalized racism
Prime Suspect 3	Runaway youth in poverty Transgender individuals Problems confronting impoverished boys with AIDS	Sexual victimization of poor boys Homophobia among police Lack of concern about boy prostitutes' sexual victimization Lack of adequate health care for AIDS victims
Prime Suspect 4: "The Lost Child"	Single working women trying to balance work and parenting; pain of abortion versus pain of balancing parenting and job Man with prison record for child sexual offense	Pressures on women regarding career advancement and family obligations; inadequate support for these efforts Stigma associated with past criminal offense leading to new crimes due to police pressure on ex-offenders
Prime Suspect 4: "Inner Circles"	Urban poor living in impoverished public housing "estates" both victimized and victimizing	Economic elites able to defraud and take advantage of poor communities and go undetected Police monitor and violently police housing estates but show favor to elite via upper-echelon connections Poor prey on each other for economic gain

Table 5.1 (cont.)

Prime Suspect Episode	Socially Marginalized Groups	Structural Roots of Individual Problems
Prime Suspect 4: "Scent of Darkness"	Tennison still undermined in her position	Police hierarchy and buddy system: undermine her investigation; appoint her organization enemy to investigate her
	Women as victims of violence	Serial killer attacks women
Prime Suspect 5: Error of Judgment	Urban poor, especially youth Victimized and victimizers in housing estates	Poor youth have few options: bad educational system and drug industry Police contain crime to estates Police disdain for estate residents Police corruption with criminal Organization
Prime Suspect 6: The Last Witness	Immigrants in London Women victims of war atrocities Hiding from victimizers Fearful of police due to immigrant status	Disrespected and stereotyped by police, politicians, and communities Do the jobs no one else wants War and ethnic cleansing using women's bodies for nationalist messages Atrocities against women ignored or denied State collaborates and protects war Criminal
Prime Suspect 7: The Final Act	Alienated youth Child sexual abuse Tennison's lack of work/life balance	Vulnerability of youth Sexual abuse most often family or close friends Alcoholism among police Tennison was married to job and faces retirement with no connections

Conclusion

As we have noted, the standard binary—evil villains versus good investigators—is a crime genre convention. The *Prime Suspect* series disrupts
this convention: some of the villains appear to be normal, law-abiding
people, and police officers are not always heroes. In some episodes even

high-ranking officers are criminals, and the police organization is sexist, racist, and anti-immigrant. Indeed, the plots reveal problems, power struggles, and changes within the police as a social institution. The diversification of police personnel leads to challenges of old hierarchies and good-old-boy (or old-lad) networks. These networks result in bad policing, corruption, and poor relations with communities of color. Tennison serves as a foil to such an organization. Consistent with arguments by Jennifer Hunt (1990), Tennison the policewoman is a symbolic danger to her male colleagues because they fear that she will expose their foibles. Sometimes Tennison is problematic in her own actions, mistreating subordinates who are women or men of color. At other times she only threatens exposure and then uses her colleagues' misdeeds as a bargaining chip.

In the *Prime Suspect* series the social dimensions that are addressed are not simply an interesting subplot but as much a part of the story as are the crimes that Tennison investigates. As Tennison traverses these social dimensions, she and the series demonstrate the relevance of these issues not only to the crimes but also to social life. There is a progressive dimension to *Prime Suspect*'s presentations of social issues. It offers glimpses of the limitations of law and the criminal justice system, and the good "guys" do not always win. Tennison is a detective in an unjust world. Sometimes she is complicit in this world, but sometimes she does what she can to produce justice amid these social injustices. But always she tries to do her job and solve crimes. In the next chapter we offer a final assessment of the strengths and weaknesses of *Prime Suspect* and compare it to other contemporary police dramas.

CHAPTER 6

Prime Suspect and Progressive Moral Fiction

As we noted in the Introduction, critics and scholars disagree about *Prime Suspect*'s success in transforming the sexist, racist, and conservative nature of most crime genre productions. In this, our concluding chapter of the book, we utilize our ideal type model of progressive moral fiction to conduct our own assessment of the transformation-containment debate surrounding *Prime Suspect* and to consider its impact on crime genre conventions and television programming. We conclude that despite its weaknesses, *Prime Suspect* has had a transformative effect on the television police crime drama. Certainly, the series enhanced the standards of the procedural's televisual sense of realism, especially forensic realism. Even more importantly, *Prime Suspect* created a space for women in television police crime drama, a subgenre that formerly tended to exclude them. We argue that *Prime Suspect* provides an example of a television series that exhibits elements of our model of progressive moral fiction. It attends to the lived experiences of socially marginalized victims and their families, connects those experiences to societal-level inequalities, challenges narrow law-and-order solutions to crime, and reveals disjunctures in the ruling apparatus of society so that viewers might see a space and hope for social change.

In the sections that follow, we will present justifications for our conclusions about the series' transformative effects but also identify ways in which *Prime Suspect* falls short in these areas. Despite their contextualization of crime and victimization within a larger social context, *Prime Suspect* episodes are ultimately concentrated on solving individual cases rather than addressing solutions to societal problems. Tennison has no

consistent ties to either a community of friends or collective change efforts. We also apply our model of progressive moral fiction to several other
contemporary police dramas, in particular *The Closer* and *The Wire*, and
compare those programs with *Prime Suspect*. The resulting analysis will
illustrate both the impact of *Prime Suspect* on the television crime genre
and the utility of our model of progressive moral fiction for media analysis
and teaching pedagogy.

Replication or Innovation?

Some scholars have commented that *Prime Suspect* incorporates many
of the conventions of the television crime genre and that its adherence to
these conventions weakens any transformative effect. Of course, common,
often formulaic elements are what define a genre. Because *Prime Suspect* is
a police drama, we expect some standard elements: a story line in which
cops capture criminals, the details of the pursuit that focus on police routines, police culture, and jargon. The criminal's capture symbolizes the
end of a threat to social order and a restoration of the status quo. Such
symbolism validates important values, for example, that crime does not
pay or at least that it should not pay. Successful genre productions are more
creative than others; they incorporate some conventions but in ways that
are fresh and interesting. John Cawleti (1976) suggests that the crime genre
presents culturally relevant images, symbols, and themes that incorporate
change even within familiar, standardized formats. Charlotte Brunsdon
(2000) sees the crime genre as a vehicle for addressing concerns such as
women's changing positions in society, social inequalities, and the changing role of police in society (see also Reiner 1994). Still, the most creative
and path-defining productions subvert conventions, add new elements,
and sometimes cross-fertilize with features from other genres. We argue
that to a greater extent than any other prior procedurals, *Prime Suspect*
explicitly and implicitly decenters male dominance of the genre. Moreover,
most of its episodes move well beyond the limited law-and-order focus of
other procedurals. Although *Prime Suspect* is neither the first nor the last
series to do so, it explores the conditions of social inequality that promote
social marginalization, crime, and victimization in ways reminiscent of
the social realism tradition.

Social Context and Social Justice

Doing justice in *Prime Suspect* is never as simple as identifying the culprit and extracting a confession. As discussed in Chapter 4, the series has altered the crime genre by occasions in which it interrogates the meaning of law and order, challenges the police organization, and engages in debates about the role of policing in society.

These broader, almost philosophical issues are addressed in story line, in dialogue, and in action. In several episodes Tennison tells other characters that she thinks the job of the police is to produce law and order. Superficially, this sounds similar to the discourses espoused in other procedurals. However, law and order do not have the same meaning for Tennison as they do for the protagonists in most traditional police dramas. In other series, law and order means catching the criminal and getting him or her to confess. As Tennison seeks the criminal, she also investigates the conditions that are the context of their criminality. Understanding their situation is necessary for understanding and solving the case. Sometimes her effort to understand the social situation generates empathy with victims, for young offenders, and for parents who do not help and even hurt their children. Even so, Tennison is a realist, not an apologist. Thus in *Prime Suspect 5: Errors in Judgment*, she understands that a boy who murdered another kid is responsible for his actions but, at the same time, had few options. She argues to the host of *CrimeNight* that kids like him have been "sucked into this violent world of street crime."

Tennison's insights into the situational aspects of crime challenge another genre convention: the role of the police. In earlier police dramas (e.g., *Dragnet*, *The Sweeney*, *Hill Street Blues*), criminals were portrayed as part of an evil mass that must be kept away from "innocent" middle-class, typically white citizens by the police. Not only does Tennison ardently oppose such containment approaches, but her investigations reveal that good and evil are not often such a simple dichotomy.

In *Prime Suspect 5: Errors in Judgment* Tennison critiques her supervisor, who advocates a containment approach to crime. She argues that the residents of low-income, predominantly black communities deserve the same police protection as that accorded to middle-class white communities. The episode depicts how this brutal environment victimizes the young drug dealer and causes larger collateral damage to others in the neighborhood. Consistent with discussions about media depictions of cosmopolitan police issues (e.g., Loader and Mulcahy 2003), *Prime Suspect* adds to the debates regarding how diverse and highly unequal communities are to be policed. *Prime Suspect* indeed introduces some of the ethical issues of policing and police organization. Tennison sometimes recognizes and tries to come to grips with her own ethical misconduct such as using innocent family members to extract a confession from her suspects (e.g., *Prime Suspect 4:* "Inner Circles"). *Prime Suspect* still stops short of addressing organizational mechanisms for improving police practice and reducing police/community conflicts.

In fact, some critics conclude that Tennison buys into the sexist, racist, and often corrupt police organization. At times, such as in *Prime Suspect 2,* in which she reinforces organizational racism against DS Oswalde, or in *Prime Suspect 3,* in which she barters silence for a promotion, complicity seems to be the case. Yet other scenes reveal that she never fully accepts the policing status quo. These scenes show her frustration with social inequality, police attitudes, and civic corruption. She sometimes circumvents these arrangements. But she is not naive, and she knows that she would fare better in her career if she could just go along. In *Prime Suspect 4:* "Scent of Darkness," after a disciplinary hearing for disobeying a superior's orders, she tells her lover: "I sat there watching them decide about *my* future, and I thought, I should be sitting there making those decisions! I fought all the bloody battles! [She sighs.] If it means working with people like Traynor or Thorndike [her organizational nemeses], I'll just have to do it, won't I." Here it appears that Tennison is acquiescing to the politics of the organization. She did not resign when brought up for discipline and resolves to get along with her organizational enemies. In the next scene, at a formal police social event, she erases her compliance. When Thorndike shares a joke with her superiors at Tennison's expense, she slings red wine on the lot of them. That action ends the episode. Thus, even when she tries to more fully buy in, Tennison often rebels at the expense of her career with the London Metropolitan Police.

Viewers can derive inspiration from Tennison's refusal to simply go along with organizational expectations for containment policing and resistance to sexism, racism, and homophobia. They can appreciate her commitment to and success in apprehending suspects despite societal and organizational obstacles. Tennison's efforts to do justice, however, are limited to the individual case. The absence of progressive organizational networking within the series leaves Tennison as an outcast and sometimes iconoclast rather than an effective agent for police organization change.

Prime Suspect and Social Realism

It may seem strange to discuss *Prime Suspect* as realism, because it is not real. It is a television program that in no way purports to be factual. In real life much of police work is boring and tedious, and crimes often remain unsolved. When they are solved, it is more frequently by citizen tips than police ratiocination (Ericson, Baranek, and Chan 1991). *Prime Suspect* does, however, evoke a televisual sense of realism that is a product of its location within the police procedural subgenre, aesthetics of production, and research into real cases and social issues.

In terms of its procedural bona fides, *Prime Suspect* offers an up-close glimpse of police routines and police culture, what Deborah Jermyn (2003, 58) calls a "fly-on-the-wall" perspective (also see Creeber 2001). Procedurals like the US series *Dragnet*, with its "just the facts, ma'am" dialogue, evoked the sense of verisimilitude that helped define the television subgenre. *Prime Suspect* takes the procedural to a new level. The series uses police jargon, overlapping dialogue, and panning shots that locate the audience in the situation room. Scenes on location take viewers to various places in a diverse country, for example, government-subsidized housing (housing estates), neighborhoods with racially and ethnically diverse populations, posh private clubs, runaway youth crash pads.

In terms of the aesthetics of production, darkly lit scenes or scenes shot in shadowy, below-ground settings—for example, the basement setting where Samira Blekic's body is discovered in *Prime Suspect 6: The Last Witness* and the parking lot where DS Otley is gunned down on a stormy night in *Prime Suspect 7: The Final Act*—yield a sense of cinematic authenticity (Jermyn 2003, 58). Glenn Creeber (2001) sees a noir sensibility to these scenes.

Prime Suspect's focus on the "unearthed body," complete with dialogue about decomposition and "the stench," or on an autopsy scene with the corpse displayed as if it is pictured in a biology textbook is a part of its procedural verisimilitude. When complaints were lodged against the series for using overly explicit visuals of dead bodies, Granada Productions

responded with a statement about its commitment to authenticity, to an
"extreme realism" (Jermyn 2003, 58–59).

Some critics (Brooks 1994) see the depiction of women's bodies in *Prime
Suspect* as voyeuristic and disempowering, but these scenes do not glamor-
ize violence. They are, rather, serious depictions of the horrifying results of
violence against women. These scenes also portray Tennison as in charge
of the investigation into the deaths of the women, and, in contrast to many
of the male detectives in *Prime Suspect* and characters in other crime genre
productions, she treats the victims with respect and importance. In the
face of the officers' disgust at the decomposition of one prostitute's body,
Tennison brushes dirt away from the corpse's face, takes a long look, and
announces, "That's Della Mornay" (their missing victim).

Beyond the respectful treatment that Tennison accords women victims,
the circumstances and social issues implied by their victimization are also
more richly developed than in most other procedurals (e.g., immigrant
experiences in *Prime Suspect 6: The Last Witness*). In part, the rich development of the episodes is facilitated by the in-depth research undertaken
by *Prime Suspect*'s production team (e.g., the depiction of women police
officers' experiences in *Prime Suspect 1*). The research grounds the crimes
and victimization of individuals within the larger sociopolitical and economic context, and, as a result, the series appears to be more thoughtful,
more realistic, and less sensational. Immigration, civic corruption, child
abuse, child prostitution, racism, and homophobia are among the issues
addressed in the series. These problems contextualize the crimes that Tennison's team investigates, and the portraits of these issues are often rich in
contrast to the superficial treatments offered in many procedurals.

Prime Suspect also raises important questions about racism, ethnic tensions, and homophobia within the police organization and community.
Prime Suspect 2 deals extensively with overt and institutional racism in
the police organization as well as Tennison's own participation in replicat-
ing racial disadvantage. Still, the series as a whole does not sufficiently
sustain the character development of men and women police officers of
color. In later episodes there is a much larger presence of white women
and people of color among the investigation teams, but their characters
are not developed in much depth, perhaps because so much focus is directed toward Tennison. People of color are featured as witnesses, victims'
family members, community members, and criminals whose characters

Prime Suspect team.

are developed as multifaceted and integral, but they are not recurring
characters in the series.

It is important to stress that *Prime Suspect* episodes provide insights into
what Tennison's talents and persistence can accomplish even in the face of
organizational and societal problems. The episodes focus on solutions to
individual crime with mere glimpses of other police team members and their
stories or the communities of which they are a part. As a result, the series
fails to inspire hopes for social change outside the criminal justice system.

Decentering Male Domination

We agree with scholars including Jermyn (2003) and Creeber (2001) that
the series has moved beyond previous programs through its plots, dialogue,
scene composition, and self-conscious reference to prior classics in ways
that transform the crime genre. The results include not only the establishment of new standards for realism in police procedurals (Jermyn 2010)
and an interrogation of notions of law, order, and justice (Cavender and
Jurik 2004) but also a significant destabilization of notions that only men
can police (Creeber 2001).

Interviews with series creator Lynda La Plante indicate that she was frustrated with the stereotyping and objectification of women in television drama and wanted to "write something better" (Day-Lewis 1998, 81). La Plante's extensive interviews and on-the-job observations of DCI Jackie Malton provided her with significant insights into the lives and work of policewomen, including their experience of discrimination (Adelman, Cavender, and Jurik 2009; Jermyn 2010).

La Plante's comments bolster Creeber's (2001) argument that Tennison's investigation of the serial murders in *Prime Suspect 1* constitutes an "explicit investigation of genre." Creeber (2001) points out interesting parallels between the name of Tennison's prime suspect in the episode, George Marlow, and the name of Raymond Chandler's chief protagonist, Philip Marlowe. As we noted earlier, George Marlow has all the outward appearances of being a nice guy, although he acknowledges his visits to the occasional prostitute. DCI Sheffard, who began the investigation, also frequented prostitutes, as do some of the detectives on his team. Thus, initially, Marlow appears to be not that different from the police team investigating him and not that different from other male detectives in prior crime genres.

Despite Tennison's struggles and setbacks throughout the series, her competence challenges traditional images of male detection prowess; her competence is rooted in her experiences as a woman, and the men's incompetence is related to their doing of masculinity (see Martin and Jurik 2007). Sheffard and his team make a number of serious mistakes in the case. Tennison, who is almost made invisible by the men in an early *Prime Suspect 1* elevator scene, takes over the case and the series (also see Jermyn 2010).

Creeber (2001) stresses the symbolic importance of a scene in which a dying Sheffard passes by Tennison as he is carried out of the station on a hospital stretcher, never to return. The visual in this scene ends with the camera on Tennison, who has an expression of realization on her face: this is her chance. Not only is the baton being passed, as Creeber (2001) suggests, but Tennison wrenches it from the hands of the Sheffards and Otleys, and, accordingly, *Prime Suspect* shifts the genre from its male-centric tradition. Tennison and *Prime Suspect* resoundingly answer Brunsdon's (2000) question of who can police: women can and do police. *Prime Suspect* has extended the boundaries of the genre, and women's place in police procedurals is now almost taken for granted in new programs (Lotz 2006).

Limitations: Is Tennison a Postfeminist Icon?

Among the criticisms of the *Prime Suspect* series and the Tennison character is the claim that Tennison is a postfeminist icon. There are several usages of the term "postfeminism," and the one that critics employ to characterize Tennison is a more negative usage. This usage refers to a perspective, often circulated by the media, suggesting that feminism has successfully achieved gender equality goals and is no longer necessary or, alternatively, that feminism is passé because it is a failed project. There is a corollary to the failed project variant: the cost to a woman of a successful career is personal unhappiness. Critics suggest that Tennison is a postfeminist icon because she is a masculinized character who mimics men police officers in appearance and behavior and she has no family or personal life outside of work. Accordingly, she represents the failure of women to be able to successfully combine work and family life, thereby sacrificing the latter for the former. We will look at the evidence for these positions in the series, but we also will employ other, more analytic usages of postfeminism to reconsider Tennison's situation as well as that of women characters in other police dramas.

Tennison as a Masculinized Character?

Scholars argue that *Prime Suspect* fails as a feminist production because Jane Tennison is a failure as a woman (Brooks 1994; Eaton 1995). She dresses in unadorned power suits and adopts a belligerent, driven, and often insensitive demeanor (Mizejewski 2004; Josephson and Josephson 2009). She can be harsh to her subordinates, and she smokes and swears like the men. When she is with colleagues and subordinates, she represses all emotion except anger at the lack of progress on a case. She is able to view dead bodies without fainting at the sight.

We disagree that these characterizations are entirely accurate portraits of the series. Tennison is also shown to have unique insights associated with being a woman (e.g., in *Prime Suspect 1*, knowledge of women's clothing and attention to details of shoe size and a victim's appearance in ways that contrast with those of the men). Moreover, her lack of emotion in front of male coworkers is shown to be a careful presentation of self, and she does show emotion once she is out of men's sight. She is shown effectively relating to women witnesses (e.g., the prostitutes in *Prime Suspect 1* whom her male colleagues have ignored or belittled).

It is true that Tennison's "performance" in front of male colleagues constructs her identity in a manner that comports with a stereotypically aggressive masculine demeanor. In those ways she conforms to hegemonic images of police masculinity. However, blanket categorizations of her as a masculinized character overlook the variety and fluidity of her gender performance in the series as a whole. More consistently accurate are characterizations of Tennison as lacking work/life balance.

Tennison and Work/Life Balance

In her analysis of *Cagney & Lacey*, Julie D'Acci (1994) notes that Christine Cagney (Sharon Gless) also was criticized by network executives for being too masculine. Their criterion for "too masculine" was that the character had no interest in marriage. Jermyn (2001) has discussed the media portrayal of Jill Dando, the host of *CrimeWatch U.K.*, who was murdered. The coverage focused on an ironic theme: Dando enjoyed professional success but lacked "real happiness" because she was unmarried. The media depict women who work outside of the home, but they also romanticize heterosexual love, motherhood, and the nuclear family and critique any threats to those supposedly "feminine" aspects of social life (see Press 1991; Dow 1996).

In the series Tennison is unable to maintain a satisfactory personal life outside of policing. She has several lovers over the course of the seven episodes, including serious attachments and other, more fleeting relationships, some with married men. In *Prime Suspect 3* an old lover, now married, seeks to renew their affair. Tennison declines to continue the relationship, telling him: "We both got what we wanted. You got married, and I got the job." Later in the episode she learns that she is pregnant, weighs the matter, and then schedules an abortion, which she has at the outset of *Prime Suspect 4*: "The Lost Child."

Indeed, the job always seems to get in the way of her maintenance of any long-term ties. Her relationship with Peter in *Prime Suspect 1* ends when he loses patience with her intense devotion to the job. She meets a new love interest, Dr. Patrick Scofield (Stuart Wilson), in *Prime Suspect 4*: "The Lost Child," but in *Prime Suspect 4*: "Scent of Darkness," she expresses her concern about screwing up her relationship with him. Then she begins to suspect that Patrick is communicating with a journalist who is publicly attacking her work. Her suspicions are untrue, and their relationship endures through the episode, but by the next *Prime Suspect* installment Tennison has been transferred. In *Prime Suspect 5: Errors of Judgment* she has an affair with her married superior, DCS Ballinger, who is corrupt and almost causes her death. There are other relationships shown or referenced in the series, but by *Prime Suspect 7: The Final Act*, Tennison is alone, isolated, and drinking heavily.

Tennison's relationships with her birth family do not fare much better. In one scene from *Prime Suspect 1* Tennison visits her parents. She is in a very good mood because it is her dad's birthday and because she has just appeared on *CrimeNight*. However, she flies into a rage when she realizes that her dad has botched the videotaping of her TV appearance. Tennison says, "Dad, you've recorded the bloody ice skating! Shit!" Her dad (Wilfred Harrison) lowers his head in shame. Peter assures her that everything is OK—he has successfully recorded the program—but Tennison responds, "No, I wanted to watch it, for Christ's sake." Her tirade is interrupted by her pager. She tears into her purse to get her mobile phone and rushes out of the room to make a call. The family is now sad. Peter says, "Maybe you'd better blow out the candles." In *Prime Suspect 6: The Last Witness* and *Prime Suspect 7: The Final Act* her father (now Frank Finlay) is dying, and she seems to come closer to him during that time. After his death she has a bitter and drunken argument with her sister, who tells her that their dad was proud of Tennison's career but that she was seldom around him. Indeed, Tennison does not appear to be a good family member. With both lovers and family, the job comes first; she is driven and committed.

Tennison fares equally poorly with her "police family." The convention in procedurals is that, although protagonists often have little home life, they still share camaraderie with their colleagues. These police family interactions are a focus in many programs (e.g., *The Gentle Touch*, *NYPD Blue*, *Cagney & Lacey*). In *Prime Suspect* there are moments when Tennison appears to be forming ties—romantic or friendship—with her police colleagues, but these ties are fleeting. Most often, if she is not on the job, she is shown leaving work or at home alone. Her romance with Oswalde in *Prime Suspect 2* goes awry and then appears to become a friendship in the later parts of the episode, but he is transferred at the end. As noted earlier, another romance, this one with her corrupt supervisor, DCS Ballinger, in *Prime Suspect 5* almost ends in her death. This relationship is particularly disheartening because he was the first supervisor who strongly supported her on the job.

A recurrent member of Tennison's investigative teams, DI Richard Haskons (Richard Hawley), who appears in *Prime Suspect* episodes 1–4, appears as her most trusted colleague. He seems generally supportive and to trust her judgment. She sometimes invites him to have a drink after work, but he always declines in order to care for his young twins. A scene in *Prime Suspect 4*: "Scent of Darkness" shows him talking on the phone to Tennison and caring for his twins; he is balancing work and family, but she is not. Ironically, it is one of her chief opponents from *Prime Suspect 1*, DS Bill Otley, who becomes loyal to her in *Prime Suspect 3* and then returns to befriend and support her through her father's death and efforts to stop drinking in *Prime Suspect 7: The Final Act*. Even this relationship is short-lived: he is killed before the end of the program. This was, sadly, the last role for actor Tom Bell, who played Otley in three *Prime Suspect* episodes (1, 3, and 7); he died in 2006, the year the final episode aired.

Thus, in the realm of work/life balance, the Tennison character does convey a sense of the failure of some women to manage both a successful job and a fulfilling personal/family life. These aspects of the *Prime Suspect*

Tennison is horrified by the murder of DS Otley.

Tennison's excessive drinking begins to interfere with her work.

series are troubling in terms of promoting positive media images of work-ing women, but they are also realistic to some extent given the challenges that women face when balancing a high-pressure job in a male-dominated field with personal and family life.

Tennison's isolation and heavy drinking are consistent with many icono-clastic protagonists in past crime fiction (Mandel 1984; Thomson 1993) and also common in police work given the stressors that often produce family breakup and alcoholism (Martin and Jurik 2007). However, the absence of social connections in Tennison's life is consistent with the type of postfeminist discourse that raises anxieties concerning women's ability to have both a meaningful career and a fulfilling personal life.

While it is easy to understand that a woman in Tennison's position would have a difficult time befriending the men in her department, it might be possible for such a character to develop relationships with other women. Yet Tennison is almost never shown to have any friendships with women, either police or nonpolice. The only time we see her doing anything social with women is in *Prime Suspect 1* when she is coming back from lunch with WPC Havers and later when she has a pint with the prostitutes.

Her lack of support for and sometimes outright hostility to policewomen subordinates is a problematic dynamic in *Prime Suspect*. Critics cite this element of the series as evidence that the mere presence of a woman does not insure a progressive, feminist program. These dynamics also contain complexities and nuances. Tennison is highly demanding and seems to cut no special breaks for the women on her team, but if they perform well and persevere, she supports them. In *Prime Suspect 4*: "Inner Circles," when DS Christine Cromwell makes a serious mistake in her work, Tennison tells her, "If you're looking for any favors, you're looking in the wrong place. One more and you're out." It seems that things might go badly between Tennison and Cromwell, but as Cromwell's performance improves, Tennison keeps her on the team despite pressure from superiors to remove her.

Another example of Tennison's relations with women subordinates comes from *Prime Suspect 5: Errors in Judgment*. Tennison, still smarting about her transfer from London to Manchester, becomes angry when DI Clare Devanney (Julia Lane) fails to relay the significant results of an informant interview. Tennison is already frustrated with the team's lack of progress and proceeds to dress her down in front of the other officers. Tennison rhetorically asks Devanney and then looks at the rest of the team: "Are you not capable of the basic procedures of investigation? You have to keep me informed." The other detectives, embarrassed, avert their eyes. In a subsequent scene, still frustrated with her team's performance, Tennison fires a barrage of questions at the other detectives, who have no answers or are afraid to answer. DI Devanney stands and ticks off the answer to each of Tennison's questions. Devanney's response is detailed and professional; we assume it mirrors the way a DI Jane Tennison would have answered years before.

Later, Tennison overhears Devanney at a restaurant holding forth with her colleagues. She mimics Tennison's "are you incapable . . ." question and then goes on, still mimicking Tennison, to say, "And me, I've screwed my way to the top," but abruptly stops when she realizes that Tennison is nearby. When Tennison returns to her own table, DCS Ballinger senses a change in her mood and asks if everything is OK with her team. Despite her anger, Tennison covers the team with a clipped "Everything is fine, just fine." Then, ironically, Ballinger tells Tennison, "Clare Devanney came straight into my office and personally asked to work under you. . . . You're a role model, Jane . . . an icon on the force." Tennison is obviously pleased, but her interactions with Devanney remain rocky until they resolve their differences late in the episode.

A final example that ultimately turns out negatively for both Tennison and her subordinate comes from *Prime Suspect 6: The Last Witness*. Tennison, who is working late at the office, glances out a window and sees DC Lorna Greaves, an African Caribbean woman officer, lovingly greet her husband and children as they arrive to drive her home from work. Tennison looks almost wistfully at Greaves and her family. She also sees Greaves arrive late for work one day. In another scene shortly thereafter, Tennison icily suggests to Greaves that she may not have the necessary commitment to work on a murder investigation team. Greaves responds that she has fulfilled every assignment on the investigation. Tennison answers that the job requires more intense commitment to the work. Greaves threatens to file a grievance claiming that Tennison is discriminating against her because she is the mother of two small children. Tennison has made an enemy with this exchange. Later, Greaves tells Tennison's superior that she has continued to work on aspects of the case that were declared off-limits due to the Official Secrets Act. As a result, Tennison is removed from the case.

Tennison's initial wistfulness and then jealousy seem to reinforce a negative version of the concept of postfeminism: her devotion to work has turned Tennison into a bitter woman; she is even harsh with other women, and this is made worse because Greaves may be experiencing the pressures associated with being a woman of color in the police organization.

There are no recurring women police officers in the series whose characters are sufficiently developed so as to present a more consistent and diverse array of character presentations—for example, those with successful family and friendship ties and those without. Because the *Prime Suspect* series is so strongly built around one character, such ensemble casts have been precluded. Sydney-Smith (2009) also suggests that the women's buddy series popularized in America by *Cagney & Lacey* and other nonpolice genre programs has never been a popular form for British television, although we do see some limited camaraderie in the more recent British series *Murder Investigation Team* (2003–5). Tennison is an isolated character who is mostly surrounded by men. She is not shown to have any recurrent or fulfilling friendship, family, or community connections.

Prime Suspect 7: The Final Act is perhaps the episode that appears most negative about Tennison's ability to have both a successful career and a satisfying personal life. We were warned at a conference by two feminist British fans who had already seen the episode in the UK that we would not like it. Indeed, there were so many fan complaints in the UK that the scriptwriter took the unusual step of defending the final episode in the *Guardian* (see Everhart 2006). Series creator Lynda La Plante also criticized the finale (Hale 2010). Perhaps not since Sir Arthur Conan Doyle killed off Sherlock Holmes at the Reichenbach Falls has the end of a crime series generated such fan discontent. *Prime Suspect 7: The Final Act* portrays Tennison on her last case before retirement and trying to locate a teenage girl reported missing by her parents. The girl has been murdered. Tennison is alone, completely alienated from family and drinking heavily to the point that she seems to have lost her professional edge. She attempts to befriend a young girl who is a witness in the case and as a result of this attachment fails to see that the girl is the killer. To many viewers, this episode may appear as the ultimate postfeminist nightmare.

Tennison is dismayed when she realizes that her young friend Penny is the killer.

However, it is important to discuss other, more positive analytic uses of the postfeminist concept in this analysis. Lotz (2001) enumerates several aspects of postfeminism that make it a useful tool for analyzing television programs. Postfeminist analytic perspectives can direct attention to narratives in programs that challenge second-wave portraits of women as unified and consistent. Postfeminism is about exploring the diversity and contradictions of women's experiences, including their diverse relations to power and to narratives that deconstruct gender and sexual binaries. In this light, postfeminist narratives serve to dramatize on television a range of contemporary struggles faced by women since the heyday of second-wave feminist activism in the 1960s and 1970s (Lotz 2001, 115–16).

Accordingly, Lotz's conceptualization would challenge the merits of asking the question of whether Tennison is masculine or feminine. This more analytic definition of postfeminism coupled with further knowledge of the real-world experiences of today's women police officers offers a more insightful reading of some of the *Prime Suspect* scenes just described. For example, the writer of *Prime Suspect 6: The Last Witness* has discussed his desire to show the tensions between Tennison's generation of police officers, who felt pressure to forgo family commitments, and the newer generation of policewomen, who have more access to family leave and other supportive family arrangements (accompanying commentary with *Prime Suspect 6: The Last Witness* DVD). The exchange between Tennison and Greaves demonstrates a difference between the two generations of policewomen. Tennison's success would have occurred because she was an organizational warrior and because of her relentless commitment to the job. Greaves would have had to confront some of the same job pressures as Tennison but also would have enjoyed somewhat more supportive policies than those available to officers of Tennison's era. As noted above, we see DI Richard Haskons doing child care in his home. Yet Tennison knows that if her team is late or distracted and the case goes badly, she will be held accountable.

Moreover, our interviews plus those of Silvestri (2003) indicate that many of the pressures for 24/7 work commitments are indeed still a part of the job. Silvestri's (2003) findings suggest that these conditions have worsened in recent years due to police budget cutbacks. Women continue to struggle to combine family and police work. Our respondents and other research studies (e.g., Brown and Heidensohn 2000) report that the demands of the job, especially at higher echelons, have prompted many policewomen to forgo applications for promotion.

Consistent with this more analytic use of the term *postfeminist*, we regard blanket categorizations of Tennison either as a "failed woman" or as "masculine" to be problematic and essentialist arguments. Such categorizations assume that particular personality characteristics and behavior are universally associated with male or female sex categories. Men are aggressive and profane, and they smoke and drink. Women should be sociable and good in the kitchen; their family should come before the job; also, they do not smoke and drink. We regard gender as a more fluid and dynamic outcome of social situations and media productions. A "doing gender" approach acknowledges the importance of gender-appropriate expectations of behavior but also recognizes that these expectations vary across organizational settings and situations (see West and Zimmerman 1987; Martin and Jurik 2007). So a woman in a predominantly male organization might choose to behave in a fashion that combines ideals of so-called masculine personality characteristics with other behaviors that are associated with traditional notions of feminine personality characteristics. We argue that Tennison, a policewoman in a traditionally male occupation, "does gender" in such a manner so as to combine culturally hegemonic notions of masculine behaviors (e.g., smoking, drinking, swearing, aggressive pursuit of her career over family) with culturally emphasized feminine behaviors (e.g., haircut, makeup, dress style, sexual attractiveness). This gender-blending dimension in *Prime Suspect* is consistent with social science research on the strategies adopted by real women in policing (Brown and Heidensohn 2000; Martin and Jurik 2007; also Jurik 1988).

It is impossible for one female character to embody the richness and diversity of all women's experience. Thus, any one character is likely to fail a "true feminist" test on at least some dimensions. What is more important is to have a wider range of women characters on the television screen to capture more of this range of experience. Lotz (2006) argues that by the late 1990s and early 2000s, a far greater array of women characters emerged on television programs, and many programs today portray working women in diverse and complex ways. Television's working women varied more by job and family situation, and they featured more varied life problems than ever before. Although working-class women and women of color were still underrepresented as central characters in television dramas, and some women characters are still portrayed in superficial and sexualized stereo-typical ways, working women, including the women in law enforcement organizations, are now taken for granted to the point that sexism is no longer a driving component of the television narratives. We will examine a few of these programs in the next section.

Comparison with Other Police Procedurals

Consistent with Lotz's argument, we find an array of women characters in contemporary police dramas. In some programs, women continue to play ill-developed or stereotypical characters reminiscent of most women's roles in 1970s policing programs. We will highlight several programs here that offer interesting parallels or contrasts with the character of Jane Tennison. These programs in no way represent the range or full complement of women's roles in police programs, but they do offer some illustrations of other contemporary police dramas and women's place in them. We will briefly discuss four programs and then provide a more in-depth discussion of two additional programs.

The UK's police procedural *Blue Murder* (2003–9) presents DCI Janine Lewis (Caroline Quentin) as its protagonist. Lewis frequently encounters work/life balance issues such as a philandering husband, an unruly son, and child care for her kids when she is called out on a case late at night (a convenient neighbor watches the children). She throws her husband out and becomes a single working mom. A man in her squad is romantically interested in her, but she declines. Later, she also declines her ex-husband's bid to reconcile. There are sometimes problems with her children, and at one point she has to take time off to deal with these. The cases that she investigates are not as realistically or as intensely depicted as in *Prime Suspect*, and they delve less deeply into social issues. This is likely at least partially related to the relatively shorter length of each *Blue Murder* episode. Lewis rarely confronts the sort of sexism that plagued Tennison. Indeed, her mainly male subordinates and superiors are fairly accepting and cordial to her. Although Lewis does not seem to have many recurrent contacts with women work colleagues, she does maintain a close friendship with a female neighbor/confidante and friendships with male colleagues. Lewis clearly experiences pressures and politics at work and challenges with work/life balance. Unlike Tennison, she has relatively stable connections both at work and at home. Her workplace stress seems to reflect that endured by anyone—man or woman—in her position. She typically solves cases by the book, and neither police organization issues nor social contexts of crimes are developed to the extent they are in *Prime Suspect*.

The UK's *Murder Investigation Team* (2003–5) features two women detectives who display some camaraderie. This program is particularly interesting because in the first season the women lead characters exhibit sharply contrasting personalities. One of the protagonists, DI Vivien Friend (Samantha Spiro), is tough, rational, and virtually emotionless in demeanor. Her colleague, DC Rosie MacManus (Lindsey Coulson), plays the kinder, gentler investigator. Friend has few connections and is not well liked by colleagues; MacManus, a mother, is liked by coworkers and relates well to suspects. The series, which adopted the aesthetics of procedural realism, is hard-hitting and contains lots of action but is generally lacking in much social commentary and does not offer more than a superficial and often sensationalizing treatment of criminals and social issues.

In the United States, *Law & Order: Special Victims Unit* (*SVU*) features a woman/man detective team, Olivia Benson (Mariska Hargitay) and Elliot Stabler (Christopher Meloni), heading up an ensemble charged with investigating violent crimes against women and children. Stories follow an ostensibly feminist narrative of the sources of violence against and by women; they address such topics as war crimes against women, anorexia, black men wrongly accused of rape, and women whose stories of rape are ignored. There is also some reversal of gender stereotypes in the series wherein the male detective, Stabler, is married and draws on his insights from being a parent to resolve cases. In contrast, Benson, the woman detective, is portrayed as a feminist who has little if any personal life outside of work and does not relate closely to women colleagues. Benson converts Stabler to a more feminist view of violence against women; he is increasingly able to relate to this view because he has daughters. Despite the series' overt feminist and topical realism, *Law & Order: SVU* has been criticized for latent misogynistic messages. Scholars argue that the series overrepresents the violent victimization of men and fails to adequately represent the violent victimization of women of color (Brito et al. 2007). In-depth content analyses of series plot and resolution find that *Law & Order: SVU* lays much of the blame for men's violence against women on female relatives of the male perpetrators, especially on mothers who have somehow damaged their sons. These sons are shown to later victimize women (Cuklanz and Moorti 2006).

Another US series, *In Plain Sight* (2008–11), also features a man/woman partnership and reverse gender stereotypes. The team works as federal marshals in a witness relocation program. The woman marshal, Mary Shannon (Mary McCormick), is not interested in a traditional version of femininity, for example, wearing makeup or forming emotional connections. She is depicted as being something of an aggressive, insensitive, and sometimes crass character. Work/life balance issues are pending because, in season 4, she is divorced and pregnant. Her partner, Marshall Mann (Frederick Weller), is more sensitive and tries to help Mary come to grips with her emotions and upcoming parenting issues.

We selected two US television series to review in a bit greater depth— *The Closer* and *The Wire*. Each provides a unique source of comparison/ contrast with *Prime Suspect*.

The Closer

Colleagues who knew that we were analyzing the *Prime Suspect* series frequently suggested that we should watch *The Closer* (Turner Network Television, 2005–). They characterized it as a US *Prime Suspect*. Scholars including Josephson and Josephson (2009), who have analyzed *The Closer*, refer to *Prime Suspect* as its "forebearer," and the series lead, Kyra Sedgwick, acknowledges Helen Mirren's performance as a pathway to her program's success. Sedgwick plays Deputy Police Chief Brenda Leigh Johnson, who is assigned to head the Los Angeles Police Department's (LAPD) Priority Murder Squad. The backstory is that her assignment is intended to produce two needed reforms: tighten up the squad's adherence to legal procedures and inculcate an awareness of cultural and racial/ethnic diversity among the detectives on the squad.

Early in her tenure as head of the unit, Johnson experiences the sort of opposition and sabotage from male subordinates and men in other units that Tennison experienced in *Prime Suspect 1*. Like Tennison, Johnson is unpopular because she is a woman but also because she is an outsider to the LAPD; she was brought in from Atlanta, Georgia, to head the unit. Johnson resembles the sort of quirky characters who sometimes populate the crime genre. Some of these quirks are cast as stereotypes of women.

In contrast to Tennison's carefully styled shorter haircuts and earth-tone business suits, Johnson wears brightly colored dresses and casual clothes to work; she has long, flowing hair that she sometimes draws back in a ponytail. At first she is unable to drive a car and later always gets lost; she secretly binges on candy; she is obsessed with her cat. Along these lines, she appears as a *Columbo*-type character. Like Lieutenant Columbo (Peter Falk), Johnson sometimes "plays dumb" and stereotypically weak, using her southern accent to lull suspects into making mistakes that help her resolve a case and gain a confession.

The Johnson character exemplifies Lotz's analytic concept of postfeminist programming wherein women characters exhibit a complex and multifaceted persona that blends traditional notions of both feminine and masculine stereotypes. Her identity is fluid and contradictory. Thus, Johnson displays the stereotypical feminine characteristics just described, but, at the same time, she is totally focused, the height of rationality, and relentlessly aggressive when she interrogates suspects; she misses nothing. She drives the team to utilize systematic empirical and scientific crime-solving techniques rather than their hunches. At times, she is a southern belle who has to be cared for (by some members of her squad and later by her lover), but in other instances, she manipulates this persona to elicit incriminating admissions or confessions. Josephson and Josephson (2009) argue that Johnson was an outsider (i.e., a CIA-trained woman from the southern United States rather than from Los Angeles) who represents the police force's need for diversification and improved attention to proper criminal procedure (especially in the wake of the O. J. Simpson trial, the Rodney King riots, and the Ramparts police scandals in LA). Although it is clear from the initial episodes of the first season that Johnson stresses these issues to her team, it is also the case that, as the seasons progress, she increasingly uses ethically questionable tactics to gain confessions and to cover for the wrongdoing of her detectives. She demeans subordinates who allow suspects to "lawyer up," and the occasions upon which clients in her interrogations are actually accompanied by counsel are few and far between.

Like Tennison, Johnson is shown to be a workaholic with work/life balance problems. Early in the first season, she indicates a preference for being unencumbered by any serious romantic interest. Later, she becomes romantically involved with an FBI agent, Special Agent Fritz Howard (Jon Tenney), and they eventually marry. As a part of the backstory, Johnson had an earlier affair with her current LAPD supervisor. At times, this becomes a problematic issue, especially for her love life. Howard does most of the housekeeping and cooking, as Johnson is a slob at home. He is often angry at her because she fails to show up for dinner and often uses trickery to get work-related information from him in order to solve one of her cases. She sometimes avoids her family but at other times draws support from them over the telephone. During one season, she takes in a family member who needs a place to live, and it is Howard who finally demands that the troubled niece return home to her parents.

After the first season, the opposition to Johnson because she is a woman decreases. Although the men are opposed to Johnson at the beginning of the first season, by season's end they are supportive of her. In an early episode, all of her squad members request transfers out of her unit. By the end of that season, when Johnson is under siege by a competitor in another department, every member of her squad threatens to resign if she is sacked. Recall that a similar reversal occurred in *Prime Suspect 1*. The *Closer*'s primary cast is comprised of actors (mostly men) drawn from various racial and ethnic populations. Because of Johnson, they cohere as a team. Like Tennison, Johnson has no enduring close connections to women colleagues or friends. After her first season, she confronts a new nemesis who is a woman from a police internal investigation unit. The two women repeatedly clash over turf in several episodes. Beyond an occasional woman assigned to her investigative team, characters that are not well developed, Johnson, like Tennison, is surrounded by men.

The Closer exhibits far more humor in its episodes than does *Prime Suspect*. Many of the plot situations entail ironic twists. For example, in one episode an extremely traditional and macho member of the team brings in his former police partner, who has retired to work a case. The sergeant is shocked to see that his former male partner has undergone a sex change to become a woman. The two must resolve their differences and work together to solve a murder.

Sometimes social issues (e.g., life in gang-ridden neighborhoods) contextualize an episode. Even so, these issues are kept at a distance. Although crimes are often committed in the context of topical social issues, the program seldom attends to these issues in much detail. Again, this may be in part related to the conventional time slot of *The Closer* when compared to *Prime Suspect* episodes. The predominant focus of episodes is on identifying the culprits and bringing them to confess. Critiques of the justice system in the series typically focus on the problems caused by excessive bureaucracy, jurisdictional squabbles, and requirements to safeguard the rights of criminal suspects. In this regard, we would describe *The Closer* as a more typical US police crime drama that is less focused on issues of social realism and adopts a more traditional law-and-order perspective.

Lotz (2006) argues that the prominence of cable as opposed to network television has opened up a space for women in lead roles. For a time, *The Closer* was the highest-rated cable program. Although relative to *Prime Suspect* the program is more limited in locating crime and victimization within some larger social context, it offers a far more multifaceted and nuanced view of a successful woman protagonist and of her attempts at work/life balance. The audience sees a highly successful woman police investigator whose personality is fluid and complicated in ways that overtly challenge the dichotomies between stereotypical masculine and feminine qualities. The humor in the episodes offers an insightful and sometimes fun look at problems with gender, racial, and sexual orientation stereotypes.

The Wire

The second program that we consider for an in-depth comparison with *Prime Suspect* is *The Wire* (HBO, 2002–8). We selected *The Wire* for analysis because in some respects it resembles *Prime Suspect*: it contains elements of the police procedural and is widely praised for its social realism and depiction of the impact of flawed institutions on the lives of its characters. Although as a weekly television series *The Wire* adheres to the convention of the one-hour format, in other ways it is an innovative program. There are continuing key players, but the series features a truly ensemble cast with in-depth portraits of characters from among the ranks of police, prosecutors, politicians, teachers, reporters, underemployed dock workers, and low-income black children in Baltimore's impoverished inner-city schools. Although police investigations figure prominently in all seasons, each season of *The Wire* focuses on a different social institution. Season 1 focuses on the Baltimore Police Department and a drug-dealing organization in western Baltimore. Season 2 focuses on the docks, the dock-workers' union, and how the severe loss of jobs pushes some dockworkers to engage in the trafficking of drugs, stolen merchandise, or immigrant women smuggled into the United States for prostitution. Season 3 focuses on Baltimore's political machine and the ways in which political corruption and subterfuge frustrate police efforts to fight urban crime and perpetuate unemployment and neighborhood decline. Season 4 focuses on the public school system as it follows the lives of three at-risk boys who live in the projects and experience limited opportunities for anything except work in the drug trade. The fifth and final season looks at the *Baltimore Sun* and identifies the organizational roots of the press's failure to cover the truth of what is going on in the city.

The Wire is focused on the institutional roots of the US urban underclass experience. Accordingly, it is the closest US television series since *Eastside, Westside* (1963–64) to resemble the British social realist tradition. It explores forces shaping the experiences of inner-city poor, street criminals, and law enforcement officials alike. For example, young black males in the projects have limited socioeconomic and educational opportunities and face considerable pressure to join the drug trade. There is strong political pressure on police to show quick results for law enforcement activities, and building cases against the leaders of powerful criminal organizations takes more time and resources than superiors are willing to allow.

On the surface, many *Wire* characters conform to popular cultural stereotypes, but continued viewing reveals myriad complexities and contradictions in their personas. The police are not always good; they are shown to be corrupt and ineffectual, willing to compromise doing what is right for career advancement. Lt. (later Maj. and Col.) Cedric Daniels (Lance Reddick) is a fast-tracker in the police organization until he becomes deeply vested in unraveling the top of a criminal drug organization. Officer James McNulty (Dominic West) is relentlessly dedicated to building a case against drug elites and is willing to challenge anyone in the department who interferes with his cases. He is a drinker and womanizer who is chronically selfish and uses others to achieve his objectives. Some of his colleagues are on the take, and they brutalize suspects. At times, the police brutality grows out of officers' frustration with their failures to control the crime problem; there is a contagion of violence that draws in otherwise good officers. While the police and politicians are a mixture of white and black characters, leaders of the drug organization and their street workers are predominantly black. D'Angelo Barksdale (Lawrence Gilliard Jr.) oversees a key territory in his uncle's drug business. He does what he has to do but is troubled by the deaths he sees in the business and by the realization that the money he earns generates neither opportunity nor respect in the larger society. Omar Little (Michael Kenneth Williams) is a tough armed robber who only targets drug dealers and their supply. He is an out gay man. In retaliation for some of his thefts, the drug organization tortures and kills his accomplice/lover. Omar, who dislikes profanity, seeks his own violent revenge against the drug organization.

At times in the series, characters and their organizations appear to have breakthroughs: police build a case and sometimes arrest drug organization leaders; young men almost leave the drug trade to pursue other life opportunities; drug addicts struggle and sometimes seem almost able to break the habit; some teachers struggle to help young boys in school; characters frequently try hard to do the right thing. Typically, however, these successes are transitory: criminal elites are arrested only to be replaced by new drug dealers; addicts relapse; kids become frustrated and rejoin the drug game; politicians fail the police and community.

The Wire has enjoyed accolades from both television critics and scholars. It is not uncommon to read newspaper reviews proclaiming that "*The Wire* is the best television program ever" (Weisberg 2006). Such reviews accompanied its run in the United States and its airing in the UK. Some reviews compare the series to Dickens's treatment of London's underclass (*Telegraph* 2009). Some critics discuss its link to previous procedurals such as *Hill Street Blues* (Moore 2010). Others describe *The Wire* as a new genre: an urban procedural whose hero is Baltimore, not its cop characters. Scholars characterize *The Wire* as conveying sociological themes and as constituting a kind of "social-science fiction" (Penfold-Mounce, Beer, and Burrows 2011).

The Wire's enthusiastic reviews mainly derive from its sense of authenticity, what one critic calls its "obsessive verisimilitude" (Weisberg 2006). This notion of realism is the theme of a Bill Moyers interview with David Simon, one of *The Wire*'s creators. Moyers says that *The Wire* "held up a mirror to an America that most of us never see" (Moyers and Simon 2011). William Julius Wilson's treatise *When Work Disappears: The World of the New Urban Poor* has been credited as inspiring the unemployed dockworkers story line. In part, *The Wire*'s realism is a function of its police procedural–like production: the characters use Baltimore slang and police jargon; the program is filmed on location; and there are references to "things Baltimore." Interestingly, another marker of the series' realism relates to the frequently mentioned credentials of its creators, David Simon, a former newspaper crime reporter, and Ed Burns, a former homicide detective. Simon's credits include a nonfiction book, *Homicide: A Year on the Killing Streets*, which generated a television series, *Homicide: Life on the Street*, and a second book and television spin-off, *The Corner: A Year in the Life of an Inner-City Neighborhood*, coauthored with Burns, his partner on *The Wire*.

If Lynda La Plante's vision for *Prime Suspect* was to give voice to the experience of London policewomen while avoiding the melodrama that had characterized past women's police dramas, the creators of *The Wire* intended for their series to address "the death of work." By this, they refer to the loss of jobs in urban America and also "the loss of integrity within our system of work" (Moore 2010). They aim to generate outrage at the social institutions that have failed the urban underclass. The series portrays the police hierarchy as being more concerned with crime statistics than with how crime affects the poor. Politicians are more worried about moving up a notch on the political ladder than helping their constituents. School-teachers "teach to the test," so that poor kids, already at a disadvantage educationally, are further disadvantaged. Newspaper reporters are more concerned with winning journalism awards than with telling the truth about the problems in Baltimore; they even falsify stories. The episodes scream with rage against these institutional failures.

The Wire very much depicts a man's world. Women constitute a small minority of the cast (only ten of the seventy-seven major characters listed on HBO's website description of cast and crew at http://www.hbo.com/the-wire/cast-and-crew/index.html). Moreover, many of the women in *The Wire* are negatively and stereotypically portrayed. City Councilwoman Marla Daniels (Maria Broom), the ambitious wife of Col. Cedric Daniels, is frustrated by her husband's lack of upward mobility and leaves him. Several actresses (not listed as main characters) play the roles of prostitutes and drug addicts. Women also play the mothers of young men in the drug trade. For example, D'Angelo's mother, Brianna Barksdale (Michael Hyatt), talks him out of negotiating with prosecutors for a shorter prison term for possession of narcotics and convinces him instead to protect his drug kingpin uncle. She does this in order to preserve her own economic welfare and position in the business. Another mother, De'Londa Brice (Sandi Mc-Cree), berates her son, Namond (Julito McCullum), for his ambivalence about a future position in the drug trade.

A few women are shown in important roles as prosecutors, journalists, and politicians. For example, Rhonda Pearlman (Deirdre Lovejoy), an assistant state's attorney, guides the police investigative team through the legal issues in their case. She also has romantic entanglements with Officer McNulty and later with Major/Colonel Daniels. Two of the most interesting and nonstereotypical women characters are Detective Kima Greggs (Sonja Sohn) and assassin Felicia "Snoop" Pearson (Felicia Pearson). Both characters are women of color. Kima Greggs is an out lesbian and a competent officer who is typically more ethical than her colleagues. Her relationship with Cheryl (Melanie Nicholls-King) shows some of the few moments of a happy family life among the police characters. Even that is fleeting: they break up after they have a baby. Greggs is teased at times about her sexual orientation, but she is generally accepted and respected by her colleagues. Felicia Pearson, who plays Snoop, is young and physically small but portrays a remorseless hit woman. She is actually someone from the streets of real-life Baltimore. As a real-life teenager, Pearson served a prison sentence for murder and recently received a sentence of three years' probation for her involvement with a Baltimore drug ring. The characters of Greggs and Snoop offer an original and nonstereotypical portrait of strong women in *The Wire*. However, these portraits are significantly outnumbered by the emphasis on the experiences and perspectives of the men who dominate the series.

The treatment of urban conditions and social institutions has prompted a lot of academic scholarship about *The Wire*. The series also has pedagogical appeal; some universities have offered courses on *The Wire*. Keffrelyn Brown and Amelia Kraehe (2011) offer a note of caution about using *The Wire* to teach about the problems facing the black community. They praise *The Wire* for troubling negative stereotypes about black masculinity and for locating black men within a political and socioeconomic context. Yet, alongside these complex portraits, the series continues to rely on stereotypes such as black man as subordinated, at-risk criminal and as forbidden, sexually desirable other. Accordingly, they suggest that those who use *The Wire* to educate students and future teachers about life in the black community must address the history and potential strengths that also reside there.

Some academic assessments of *The Wire* have been very critical. For example, Peter Dreier and John Atlas (2009) acknowledge that the series had a definite and laudable political agenda: exposing the failure of social institutions to improve the lives and situation of the urban poor. However, they conclude that although the series vividly reveals the problems, it offers no solutions. It portrays urban life as hopeless; characters are trapped in a system beyond reform. Dreier and Atlas are dismayed that the series ignores the black working class and the various low-income community movements and groups that are working (sometimes successfully) to redress the problems that the series depicts.

Anmol Chaddha, William Julius Wilson, and Sudhir Venkatesh (2008) defend the series, arguing that *The Wire* depicts the challenges of urban inequality better than any other media or scholarly presentation. They note instances where characters stepped up and acted in ways that improved the situation; for example, Bunny Colvin (Robert Wisdom) saved a schoolkid from what was seemingly an inevitable life of dealing drugs. Chaddha, Wilson, and Venkatesh conclude that, by revealing the crisis of urban inequality, *The Wire* is a valuable tool of political education that may mobilize reforms.

We agree that *The Wire* is an innovative television program that offers an important and in-depth analysis of the institutional roots of social problems. It also provides complex and dynamic portraits of law enforcement personnel, underemployed members of the working class, as well as impoverished youth and criminals. It attends to the plight of the urban poor, especially the role of the public school system, in a depth that few US television programs have ever attempted. At the same time, we agree with Dreier and Atlas (2005) that the series provides no hope because it fails to offer glimpses of collective movements fighting to address these social conditions. The black community is consistently shown as chaotic and disorganized; this represents part but not all of the real strengths that can be found in today's black cultures and communities. We also agree with Brown and Kraehe (2011) that without portraits of more instances of community resiliency, the only apparently effective solution to the urban problems depicted in *The Wire* is the removal of black youth from their communities by some external agent. Thus, although *The Wire* offers a more in-depth portrait of institutional defects than that seen in *Prime Suspect*, it also offers significantly less hope for individuals or groups to produce justice. Although compelling, the series is cynical in its hopelessness. Even a character who does good (again, Bunny Colvin, who saves young Namond from a life as a dealer) does so by removing a young man from his neighborhood. Of course, he has to, because there is no effective black community, only dealers and addicts in *The Wire*.

One element of our model of progressive moral fiction is that productions should show the audience some sense of hope and mobilize efforts to improve the situation: if a character can make a difference, maybe I can, too. Characters in *The Wire* cope as best they can, but there is little hope that they can transcend their bleak lives.

The television programs that we have discussed here exemplify some of what has happened in police crime drama since *Prime Suspect*'s inception. They demonstrate the variety of character types that are available to women but also the continued prevalence of male actors and perspectives in the crime drama. Programs vary in the extent to which they stress realism, contextualize crime and criminals, challenge narrow conceptions of justice, and offer hope for social change. *The Wire* is the most committed to social realism and to depictions of the impact of social forces on characters, but it has little place for women, and its hopelessness weighs against the possibility of justice provocateurs.

A US version of *Prime Suspect* based upon the original British series premiered in the fall of 2011 on NBC. Maria Bello plays Detective Jane Timoney. Timoney has to cope with challenges to her presence by the male police organization. She is excluded from cases by the other male detectives and struggles to advance despite considerable opposition. Despite some international interest in the series, it suffers from low ratings, so its future is uncertain.

Prime Suspect and Progressive Moral Fiction: A Final Assessment

Prime Suspect is a police procedural: Jane Tennison and her team investigate homicides and try to capture the murderers; they usually succeed. Despite its reliance on such standard conventions, *Prime Suspect* has greatly altered the television crime genre. The protagonist is a woman, which was rare on television police dramas. Perhaps the strongest indicator of *Prime Suspect*'s success is that police drama is not the same as it was before the series began more than twenty years ago. Male detectives certainly have not disappeared from television, but successful, star-driven series with women in lead roles are now a fixture in prime-time programming (e.g.,

The Closer, Blue Murder, Saving Grace), and their roles are more varied and multifaceted. After *Prime Suspect*, it would now seem almost jarring to hear dialogue wherein a character refuses to speak with a Maggie Forbes or a Jane Tennison and says instead, "I'd rather speak with a man."

We have analyzed the *Prime Suspect* series through the lens of our ideal model of progressive moral fiction. We have argued that the series offers insights into the lives of socially marginalized police officers, victims, and families. It takes a hard look at contemporary social issues of our day— sexism and racism in policing, sexual exploitation and abuse, drugs in low-income communities, immigration, and elite and police corruption. It locates the problems of offenders, victims, and police within the larger context of police organization and societal power relations. The coverage of these experiences and issues is hard-hitting and, at times, gruesome. Yet there are moments in every episode that portray fissures in ruling relations and the imperfections of the legal and criminal justice systems. From *Prime Suspect 1* through *Prime Suspect 7* we see Tennison make a difference even amidst frequent failures. For this reason, we conclude that the series contains key elements of a progressive moral fiction. Jane Tennison is often a justice provocateur, albeit a flawed one.

Even Tennison's imperfections and contradictions make the series a cultural production that can produce worthwhile public discussions and classroom teaching about social justice and gendered, racialized, and heterosexist workplace organizations and identities. Its coverage of social issues and complex portraits of gender, race, class, and sexual orientation demonstrate the potential for police procedurals to address the important issues of our day.

Yet there are still problems with the series that cause it to fail as a perfect exemplar of progressive moral fiction. Despite *Prime Suspect*'s deconstruction of white male police organizations and Tennison's success in challenging that hierarchy to do justice, the program is ultimately focused on the case at hand. Tennison observes social conditions and their impact on people in the case, but she cannot always alter those forces, nor does she connect with collectivities that can. The series lacks the in-depth coverage of social institutions offered in social realism series such as *The Wire*. And although her isolation is consistent with many past protagonists of the crime genre, it falls short of our hopes for a progressive moral fiction that can inspire viewers through glimpses of progressive and collective social and institutional change. Although the program is not as cynical as *The Wire* and offers a more in-depth treatment of social issues than that seen in *The Closer*, we often observe Tennison alone and isolated, sometimes hassling instead of helping other women police investigators.

In contrast, the real-life women police administrators with whom we spoke cited numerous examples in which women police administrators had made a difference through leadership to change the male-dominated organizational structure. Respondents cited examples of policies that they had promoted in order to improve opportunities for work/life balance. They also cited instances of camaraderie and mutual support among women officers and growing numbers of men officers. Women's police associations have formed in the UK, Europe, the United States, and Australia to disseminate information and organize women officers around professional and global social issues (Martin and Jurik 2007).

Despite our criticisms of *Prime Suspect* and the Tennison character, we do not conclude that she is emblematic of the negative side of postfeminism or that the series entirely fails to inspire progressive social change. Our favored approach in this book has been to reject such binary categorizations. Tennison is a complex character who denies us the comfort of complete success or complete failure. Her dynamic and sometimes contradictory persona exemplifies Patricia Hill Collins's (2000) analytic concept of *both/ and*. Tennison both challenges and is oppressed by the organization, and she sometimes helps and sometimes oppresses her subordinates.

For example, the last scene of *Prime Suspect 7: The Final Act* provides an ideal example of the ambiguity surrounding Tennison's character. We may wish with other fans that the last episode had been different somehow. In other ways, however, that last episode was a fitting end to the series. With the help of her former nemesis, DS Otley, she is coping with the drinking problem and has solved her last case. Tennison talks with Tony Sturdy (Gary Lewis), a grieving father whose daughter was murdered; she has solved the mystery and given his family some closure. Sturdy, who knows that Tennison is retiring, takes her hand and says, "Thank you for everything, thank you." It is as if he is thanking her not only for solving his daughter's murder but somehow for more: for the cases in her career.

In the final scene, Tennison leaves the station house for the last time, skipping the party that is in her honor. On the street, she sees a young officer hurriedly suit up for work. Tennison seems to smile slightly with some satisfaction as she takes note of the officer. She seems comfortable with herself as she walks away. Her image is clear, but the areas ahead of her are blurry in the camera frame. The ending is ambiguous: Tennison does not end in joy and romance, but neither is she wholly defeated. The future is unknown.

We agree with other scholars (Cawleti 1976; Brunsdon 2000) that the crime genre offers an opportunity to address important social issues, including crises and trends in policing and social control (see also Reiner 1994). Not only does *Prime Suspect* address important social issues, it does so in an open-ended treatment that is still unusual on television. We know from decades of media research that television viewers actively engage television texts and that the meanings they decode may be different from those that the producers encode; further, these differences may vary along the lines of age, race, social class, gender, and sexual orientation.

The lack of a resolution and the imperfections of many *Prime Suspect* episodes with regard to a progressive moral fiction offer space for dialogue and discussion. Accordingly, we argue that the *Prime Suspect* series offers an excellent pedagogical opportunity for addressing social justice issues. Cameron Luke (1993) and James Trier (2007) suggest that popular culture texts offer a "back door" for engaging students in discussions about complex theories and concepts. Yet Brown and Kraehe (2011) caution that it is essential to engage these "texts" critically, to examine implicit as well as explicit meanings, and to draw in additional historical contexts and oppositional arguments. With these caveats in mind, we argue that our model of progressive moral fiction offers a pedagogical tool for using media to address a variety of seemingly private troubles as social issues with important justice implications. These might include debates about the true nature of police work, police behavior, workplace inequalities, discrimination in the workplace, organizational corruption and change, images of white women and men and women of color on television, and problems of work/life balance. We hope that our treatment of *Prime Suspect* serves as a pathway to such analyses in the classroom and beyond.

Prime Suspect Episode Overview

Prime Suspect 1. The body of a woman, tortured, raped, and murdered, is discovered; she is identified as a prostitute. Detective Chief Inspector (DCI) John Sheffard of the London Metropolitan Police heads the investigation. George Marlow, who has served a prison sentence for violently assaulting a woman, is arrested but denies involvement. Sheffard suddenly dies, and DCI Jane Tennison asks to replace him. Although she is Sheffard's equal in rank, Tennison has not been allowed to head murder investigations. Her superior initially refuses Tennison but then, under orders from his own superiors, assigns her to the case. Sheffard's team of male detectives is incredulous that a woman will head the investigation, and they try to sabotage her. They become more incensed when Tennison reviews the case, determines that Sheffard misidentified the victim, and orders Marlow's release because of a lack of evidence. When a review of records reveals that a similar murder occurred north of London, Tennison investigates. She learns that Sheffard also headed that investigation; although the victim was a prostitute, he did not interview prostitutes who knew her. Tennison interviews these women and learns valuable information. Other victims are discovered; these are serial murders. Tennison is relentless in her attempt to find evidence against Marlow. Evidence comes from several sources: her assistant, WPC Maureen Havers, discovers that Marlow is linked to the victims through his wife; Tennison directs a stake-out that discovers the building where Marlow tortured and killed his victims. His wife, Moyra, under intensive questioning from Tennison, recants Marlow's alibi. The detectives arrest Marlow and sing Tennison's praises. The time-consuming investigation takes a toll on Tennison's personal life; she returns from the office to find that her lover has moved out.

Prime Suspect 2. The body of a young woman is exhumed from a shallow grave in an African Caribbean neighborhood. DCI Tennison heads the investigation. Because of prior incidents involving residents and the police, community members are hostile to the police. Racial tensions also are evident within the police department. Some homicide detectives, especially Detective Inspector (DI) Frank Burkin, are racist, and their further actions antagonize residents and impede the investigation. Burkin resents Detective Sergeant (DS) Bob Oswalde's assignment to the team because Oswalde is a black man. Tennison also opposes Oswald's assignment but for a different reason: he is her former lover, and she fears that discovery of their relationship could harm her career. Unable to have Oswalde removed from her team, she assigns him to menial tasks. Oswalde perseveres and generates leads: a young man, Tony Allen, knew the victim and began to exhibit behavioral problems after her death. On his own, Oswalde subjects the unstable Allen to a grueling interrogation; later, Allen hangs himself in his jail cell. The police investigate Oswalde because of Allen's death. Tennison stands by him, and they have a rapprochement. She pursues a different set of leads that implicate the nephew of a former resident of the neighborhood. She directs a stake-out that allows Oswalde to capture the nephew. Tennison's relationship with Oswalde is known by her nemesis, DCI Thorndike, who uses the information against her. She is bypassed for a promotion, and Thorndike is promoted instead. Tennison requests a transfer.

Prime Suspect 3. Colin James, a "rent boy" (a teenage prostitute with men clients), is found burned to death. Evidence points to the involvement of a violent pimp, but he has an alibi from Edward Parker-Jones, a respected community leader who manages a youth shelter. The investigation takes Tennison and the detectives into the world of teenage prostitution, pornography, and transsexual cabarets. Jessica Smithy, a journalist, tells her that James had promised to provide information about his famous clients, including a high-ranking police officer. Tennison is pressured by her superiors to narrow her investigation only to James's murder. The sexual nature of the case gives rise to numerous "fag" jokes among the detectives. One detective reveals to the team that he is a homosexual; the detectives shun him, but Tennison supports him. She learns that Parker-Jones has a history of abuse with kids but that he is well connected with the police hierarchy. She also discovers that John Kennington is a command-level officer who was linked to the young prostitute. She is pressured to protect Kennington and to end her investigation. She agrees that she will find James's killer but leave Kennington out of the investigation. In exchange, she demands that her superiors support her request for promotion. Tennison discovers that Vera Reynolds, a transsexual, thought that she had killed James, but she only knocked him unconscious. Parker-Jones set the fire that killed James so that he would not reveal his famous clients and their link to Parker-Jones. Tennison lacks the evidence to arrest Parker-Jones, so she gives Smithy her case file, knowing that the journalist will report the story and destroy Parker-Jones's career. During the case, Tennison encounters a former lover who wants to renew their romance. Although she declines to renew their affair, they do have sex, and she becomes pregnant. At the conclusion of the episode, she arranges to have an abortion. Tennison also is promoted to detective superintendent.

Prime Suspect 4 consists of three shorter episodes. "The Lost Child" opens with a scene in which Detective Superintendent Tennison has just had an abortion and is anxious to return to work. Her case is the investigation of a kidnapping. Susan Covington has been found unconscious, and her baby, Vicki, is missing. Juxtaposed with the preceding scene from her abortion, Tennison is emotionally driven to find Vicki before she is harmed. Susan reports that on several occasions she has seen a man who seemed interested in Vicki walking with two young girls. The man, Chris Hughes, has recently been released from prison for child sexual abuse. Hughes lives with Anne Sutherland, a single mother with two girls who does not know about his record. Tennison interviews Hughes's psychiatrist, Dr. Patrick Schofield, who doubts Hughes's involvement; Vicki is much younger than the other children Hughes had abused. Schofield gives Tennison a video of his interviews with Hughes. Vicki's body is discovered; she has been asphyxiated. A detective, DI Tony Muddyman, produces a crisis when he gives the video of Hughes's interviews to Anne Sutherland. Muddyman tells Tennison that he was an abused child. Hughes is taken into custody but escapes into Sutherland's house, where he holds her two daughters hostage. Tennison promises that if he releases the girls and surrenders, he will be arrested without incident. However, upon leaving the house, Hughes sees police snipers and runs back inside the house with one of Sutherland's daughters. At this point, Tennison is replaced by tactical police because of the inflamed hostage situation. Susan Covington comes to the scene and confesses to Tennison that she killed Vicki and faked the kidnapping and the attack upon herself. She had become distraught because she was a single mother trying to work and could not stop Vicki from crying.

Prime Suspect 4: "Inner Circles." Denis Carradine, manager of the exclusive Huntington Club, is found dead in his home. Tennison and her detectives, including Detective Sergeant Christine Cromwell, investigate. The club's new manager, James Greenlees, suggests that the killers are youth from a nearby low-income housing council estate. Tennison and her detectives persist in asking questions about Carradine; Greenlees complains to Tennison's superiors, who are well connected to these community elites. The investigation reveals, first, that Carradine was in financial trouble and embezzling from the club and, second, that he headed a company based in the Bahamas that had purchased a property from the housing council at an unusually low price. Carradine's solicitor, Maria Henry, is unhelpful. At an estate council meeting, residents become angry because the sale of the property seems to be fraudulent. The police are called, and a melee follows. Tennison and Cromwell, in plainclothes, are manhandled by the police; Cromwell, who is bitter about the elite corruption, loses her temper. Greenlees blames the disturbance on them, and Cromwell is singled out for disciplinary action. Tennison is ordered off the case but threatens her superior: information might be leaked to the press if she is unable to close the case. She and Cromwell are allowed to continue. Maria Henry's young daughter, Polly, sleeps with a man named Geoff, who beats her. He is murdered; witnesses saw a woman who resembled Maria Henry at the scene. She denies involvement in the murders and, as a lawyer, knows that Tennison has no conclusive evidence against her. Tennison harshly interrogates Polly Henry in Maria's presence, making it seem as if she suspects Polly of the murders. Maria confesses: she paid Geoff to kill Carradine and then told Hamish Endicott, a bartender at the club who has a crush on Polly, that Geoff raped Polly; Hamish killed Geoff. After Henry's confession, DS Cromwell congratulates Tennison for her tactics. Tennison says with regret that both she and Maria used Polly.

Prime Suspect 4: "Scent of Darkness." A woman is murdered in a manner that resembles the serial killings for which George Marlow was convicted in episode 1. Similar killings follow; the method of the crimes suggests Marlow's innocence. A book by Mark Whitehouse argues that Tennison arrested the wrong man. The police assign Tennison's nemesis, Thorndike, to reconsider the original murders; he recommends reopening the original cases. Tennison is removed from the new cases, but her friend DI Richard Haskons continues to share case details with her. She discusses the possibility of a copycat killer with her new lover, Dr. Patrick Schofield, whom she met during "The Lost Child" episode. He discovers amid her Marlow file that those victims, like the current ones, were doused with a gardenia-scented perfume. Tennison did not recall this detail, the media did not report it during the early murders, and it is not in Whitehouse's book. After overhearing a phone message on Schofield's answering machine, Tennison becomes suspicious that he is in contact with Whitehouse, the writer; she breaks up with him. She visits Marlow's mother and learns that the woman had an affair during Marlow's youth, that he discovered the affair and was upset about it, and that she used a gardenia perfume in those days. Tennison visits Marlow in prison and is suspended from her job for the unauthorized visit, especially after having been removed from the case. Haskons is convinced that the focus on the old cases is misguided and convinces his superior that they are on the wrong path; they shift tactics, and their investigation reveals that one of Marlow's prison guards, Len Sheldon, has purchased gardenia perfume. They track him down before he can kill his latest victim. Sheldon had met Marlow's wife, Moyra, during a prison visit. They had a relationship, and she revealed the secret of the gardenia perfume to him. He began the copycat killings to see what it felt like to be Marlow. Tennison and Schofield reconcile. At the conclusion of the episode they are at a police social event. She dances with Thorndike, but afterward he shares a joke with his high-ranking friends. Tennison, angered because she thinks these men are laughing at her, slings wine on them.

Prime Suspect 5: Errors of Judgment. Tennison, recently transferred to Manchester, speaks at a public school heavily populated by poor children of color. She is emotionally touched by a student named Campbell Lafferty. Later, she is called to oversee an evolving situation: Nazir Ahmed has been shot to death, and another young man is holed up in the low-income housing estate where Ahmed was killed. A local crime boss nicknamed "The Street" appears and against Tennison's orders brings out Michael Johns, the youth who was wounded in the gunfire that killed Ahmed. No weapons are found at the scene. Tennison and her team, including DI Clare Devanney, investigate. Devanney interviews Ahmed's girlfriend, who says that he was a drug runner and was siphoning off profits from his supplier. Tennison reprimands Devanney for failing to share this information. Tennison has dinner with her superior, DCS Martin Ballinger. They discuss crime strategies, and he shares with her his containment view: his goal is to insure that drugs and crime remain in the poor parts of the city and away from the decent, law-abiding people. Tennison characterizes his strategy as ghettoization. After dinner, they have sex. Tennison has several run-ins with The Street but learns nothing. He seems to be one step ahead of her; she thinks he has an informant among the detectives and suspects Devanney. After Michael Johns is released from the hospital, he visits his girlfriend, Janice Lafferty. Her brother, the youth whom Tennison met during her school talk, storms out of the apartment, goes to the police station, and confesses to killing Ahmed. Tennison doubts this and releases him. Later a machine gun is found with his fingerprints on it, and a witness confirms that Lafferty killed Ahmed. He was trying to kill Michael Johns to keep him away from Lafferty's sister but killed Ahmed by mistake. The Street makes Johns kill Lafferty for interfering with his criminal operations. Tennison learns that DCS Ballinger worked an earlier case that involved The Street, who was not convicted due to procedural errors. The police arrest Johns, who admits that The Street ordered him to kill Lafferty. He tells Tennison that he fears for Janice Lafferty's safety. The Street kidnaps Janice before Tennison can save her. Tennison learns where The Street is holding Janice and arrives there before the other detectives. He is about to kill Tennison when Ballinger arrives. An exchange reveals that Ballinger and The Street worked together as a part of Ballinger's containment model. The Street threatens Ballinger, and police snipers kill him.

Prime Suspect 6: The Last Witness. The tortured body of a young woman is discovered at a construction site. She is Samira Blekic, a Bosnian refugee. Amid a general backdrop of anti-immigrant sentiment politically and also among the police, Tennison pulls rank over her subordinate, DCI Simon Finch, and takes over his investigation. The medical examiner concludes that Samira's torture corresponded with much older torture marks. Acting on a tip, Tennison discovers Samira's sister, Jasmina, hiding in a secret compartment under an apartment floor. Jasmina confides that she and Samira escaped to London after being raped and tortured years earlier by a sadistic paramilitary commander, Dragon Yankovic; others were massacred. Through CCTV tapes, DC Lorna Greaves sees that another Bosnian, Duscan Zigic, was at the construction site where Samira was found. He is questioned with the aid of Milan Lukic, an optician who works as a police interpreter. Zigic is unhelpful and is released. The detectives discover more evidence against Zigic, but before they can arrest him, he murders Jasmina. When Tennison reports the Bosnian massacre, she is called to a meeting with an MI6 agent. The agent denies that a massacre occurred and warns Tennison that she is now forbidden by the Official Secrets Act from investigating the Blekic murders. After reviewing interview tapes, Tennison suspects Lukic, the interpreter. She visits him under the guise of getting an eye examination and becomes more suspicious. She enlists a former lover, Robert West, a journalist with expertise in Bosnia. He discovers a video of the massacre. They travel to Bosnia, see the massacre site, and learn about Dragon Yankovic. Back in London, Tennison reprimands DI Lorna Greaves, who reports to their superior that Tennison is pursuing the investigation. Tennison is removed from the case but receives updates from DCI Finch. She tells Lukic's wife that he was having an affair and secretly records the wife's angry admission that Lukic is an MI6 informant. Tennison plays the tape to Zigic, who admits that he and Yankovic murdered the real Lukic and that Yankovic assumed his identity. Zigic tells Tennison where Lukic is buried. She arrests Yankovic for murdering Lukic, a crime for which he enjoys no Official Secrets protection. Tennison and West break off because he provided Bosnians with her case information that Lukic was Yankovic, and they kidnap him, planning to return him to Bosnia.

Prime Suspect 7: The Final Act. Detective Superintendent Jane Tennison is at a low ebb: she is retiring, her father is dying in a hospital, and she has become an alcoholic. She is assigned to her final case, which involves Tony and Ruth Sturdy, who are worried because their daughter, Sallie, is missing. Tennison and her detectives interview Sallie's contacts as they search for her. Sallie was linked to a young man, Curtis Flynn, whom Tennison cannot locate. Sallie also is linked to a friend, Penny Phillips, age fourteen, and Penny's father, Sean Phillips, the headmaster of her school. Tennison befriends Penny, and the girl resonates with her. As Tennison investigates the world of teenage crash pads, her father dies. Following his funeral, she has a drunken encounter with her sister and niece. Tennison's drinking is interfering with her work, so she attends Alcoholics Anonymous meetings, where she encounters another officer, DS Bill Otley, a man who has been both her adversary and her supporter over the years; he helps her with her father's death and her drinking. However, as Otley and Tennison leave the hospital, Flynn shoots and kills Otley. Flynn kidnaps Penny and takes her to his sister Rosalie's apartment, but she escapes. Sallie's body is discovered in a wooded area; she has been stabbed to death. Tennison's interactions with Tony Sturdy are bad because her drinking causes an insensitive interview and because she has reason to doubt his alibi for the period when Sallie went missing. In turn, Tony suspects Sean Phillips. Tennison sees a video that shows Sean Phillips interacting with Sallie in a manner that suggests a sexual relationship. Indeed, Sallie was pregnant by Phillips. Penny knew this and killed Sallie out of jealousy over her father. Penny loses control and threatens Tennison's niece; the police arrest Penny, who confesses. Tony, knowing that Tennison is retiring, thanks her for bringing the case to a conclusion. As her coworkers revel at her retirement party, Tennison avoids them, quietly leaves the station house for the last time, and walks away.

References

Abercrombie, Nicholas. 1996. *Television and Society*. London: Polity Press.

Adelman, Madelaine, Gray Cavender, and Nancy Jurik. 2009. "The Life and Times of Jane Tennison of the London Metropolitan Police: Crusader for Justice or Post-Feminist Icon?" In *Women, Violence and the Media*, edited by Drew Humphries, 175–96. Boston: Northeastern University Press.

Aiken, Jane. 1997. "Striving to Teach 'Justice, Fairness, and Morality.'" *Clinical Law Review* 4(1): 1–64.

———. 2001. "Provocateurs for Justice." *Clinical Law Review* 7(2): 287–306.

Allen, K. 1997. "A Study of the Career Progression of Male and Female Police Officers in Bedfordshire." PhD diss., Birkbeck College, University of London.

BBC. 2004. "Portraying Real People on Screen." *Women's Hour*. January 13. http://www.bbc.co.uk/radio4/womanshour/12_01_04/tuesday/info3.shtml.

Benshoff, Harry, and Sean Griffin. 2009. *America on Film: Representing Race, Class, Gender, and Sexuality at the Movies*. 2nd ed. New York: Blackwell Publishing.

Bird, Elizabeth, and Jonathan Godwin. 2006. "Film in the Undergraduate Anthropology Classroom: Applying Audience Response Research in Pedagogical Practice." *Anthropology and Education Quarterly* 37(3): 285–99.

Blum, Denise. 2006. "Expanding the Dialogue: A Response to Bird and Godwin's 'Film in the Undergraduate Anthropology Classroom.'" *Anthropology and Education Quarterly* 37(3): 300–306.

Breu, Christopher. 2005. *Hard-Boiled Masculinities*. Minneapolis: University of Minnesota Press.

Brito, Sarah, Tycy Hughes, Kurt Saltzman, and Colin Stroh. 2007. "Does 'Special' Mean Young, White and Female? Deconstructing the Meaning of 'Special' in *Law & Order: Special Victims Unit*." *Journal of Criminal Justice and Popular Culture* 14(1). http://www.albany.edu/scj/jcjpc/vol4is1/britto/pdf.

Brooks, Dianne. 1994. "Television and Legal Identity in Prime Suspect." *Studies in Law, Politics and Society* 14:89–104.

Brown, Jennifer. 1998. "Aspects of Discriminatory Treatment of Women Police Officers Serving in Forces in England and Wales." *British Journal of Criminology* 38(2): 265–82.

———. 2003. "Women Leaders: A Catalyst for Change." In *Police Leadership in the Twenty-First Century: Philosophy, Doctrine and Development*, edited by Robert Adlam and Peter Villiers, 174–87. Winchester: Waterside Press.

———. 2007. "From Cult of Masculinity to Smart Macho: Gender Perspectives on Police Occupational Culture." *Sociology of Crime, Law and Deviance* 8:189–210.

Brown, Jennifer, and J. Fielding. 1993. "Qualitative Differences and Women Police Officers' Experiences of Occupational Stress." *Work and Stress* 7:327–40.

Brown, Jennifer, and Frances Heidensohn. 2000. *Gender and Policing: Comparative Perspectives*. New York: St. Martin's Press.

Brown, Keffrelyn, and Amelia Kraehe. 2011. "Socio-Cultural Knowledge and Visual Re(-)Presentations of a Black Masculinity and Community: Reading *The Wire* for Critical Multicultural Teacher Education." *Race Ethnicity and Education* 14(1): 73–89.

Brownmiller, Susan. 1975. *Against Our Will: Men, Women and Rape*. New York: Simon and Schuster.

Brunsdon, Charlotte. 2000. "The Structure of Anxiety: Recent British Television Crime Fiction." In *British Television: A Reader*, edited by Edward Buscombe, 195–217. Oxford: Clarendon Press.

Butler, Jeremy. 2007. *Television: Critical Methods and Applications*. 3rd ed. Mahwah, NJ: Lawrence Erlbaum Associates.

Buxton, D. 1990. *From "The Avengers" to "Miami Vice": Form and Ideology in Television Series*. Manchester: Manchester University Press.

Carmody, Dianne. 1998. "Mixed Messages: Images of Domestic Violence on 'Reality' Television." In *Entertaining Crime: Television Reality Programs*, edited by Mark Fishman and Gray Cavender, 159–74. New York: Aldine de Gruyter.

Cavender, Gray, and Sarah Deutsch. 2007. "CSI and Moral Authority: The Police and Science." *Crime Media Culture* 3(1): 67–81.

Cavender, Gray, and Nancy Jurik. 1998. "Jane Tennison and the Feminist Police Procedural." *Violence against Women* 4(1): 10–29.

———. 2004. "Policing Race and Gender: An Analysis of *Prime Suspect 2.*" *Women's Studies Quarterly* 32(3–4): 211–30.

———. 2007. "Scene Composition and Justice for Women: An Analysis of the Portrayal of Detective Tennison in the British Television Program *Prime Suspect.*" *Feminist Criminology* 2(4): 277–303.

———. 2010. "Truth, Reality, Justice, and the Crime Genre: Implications for Criminological Inquiry and Pedagogy." In *International Handbook of Criminology*, edited by Shlomo Shoham, Paul Knepper, and Martin Kett, 455–81. London: CRC Press.

Cawleti, John. 1976. *Adventure, Mystery, and Romance*. Chicago: University of Chicago Press.

Chaddha, Anmol, William Julius Wilson, and Sudhir Venkatesh. 2008. "In Defense of *The Wire*." *Dissent Magazine*. Summer. http://dissentmagazine.or/article/?article=1237.

Chandler, Raymond. 1940. *Farewell My Lovely*. New York: Knopf.

———. 1946. "The Simple Art of Murder." In *The Art of the Mystery Story*, edited by Howard Haycraft, 222–37. New York: Grosset and Dunlap.

Chiricos, Ted, and Sarah Eschholz. 2002. "The Racial and Ethnic Typification of Crime and the Criminal Typification of Race and Ethnicity in Local Television News." *Journal of Research in Crime and Delinquency* 39:400–420.

Collins, Patricia Hill. 2000. *Black Feminist Thought*. 2nd ed. New York: Routledge.

Cooke, Lez. 2003. *British Television Drama: A History*. London: BFI Publishing.

Cormier, Harvey. 2008. "Bringing Omar Back to Life." *Journal of Speculative Philosophy* 22(3): 205–13.

Creeber, Glenn. 2001. "Cigarettes and Alcohol: Investigating Gender, Genre, and Gratification in *Prime Suspect*." *Television & New Media* 2(2): 149–66.

Crisell, Andrew. 2006. *A Study of Modern Television: Thinking inside the Box*. London: Palgrave/Macmillan.

Cuklanz, Lisa, and Sujata Moorti. 2006. "Television's 'New' Feminism: Prime-Time Representations of Women and Victimization." *Critical Studies in Media Communications* 23(4): 302–21.

Curti, Lidia. 1988. "Genre and Gender." *Cultural Studies* 2:152–67.

D'Acci, Julie. 1994. *Defining Women: Television and the Case of "Cagney & Lacey."* Chapel Hill: University of North Carolina Press.

Davis, Angela. 1981. *Women, Race and Class*. New York: Random House.

———. 1999. *Blues Legacies and Black Feminism: Gertrude "Ma" Rainey, Bessie Smith, and Billie Holiday*. New York: Vintage.

Day-Lewis, Sean. 1998. *Talk of Drama: Views of the Television Drama "Now and Then."* Luton: University of Luton Press.

Deutsch, Sarah, and Gray Cavender. 2008. "CSI and Forensic Realism." *Journal of Criminal Justice and Popular Culture* 15:34–53.

Dick, Penny, and Catherine Cassell. 2004. "The Position of Policewomen: A Discursive Analytic Study." *Work, Employment and Society* 18:51–72.

Dobash, R. Emerson, and Russell P. Dobash. 1979. *Violence against Wives: A Case against the Patriarchy*. New York: Free Press.

Dove, George. 1982. *The Police Procedural*. Bowling Green, OH: Bowling Green University Popular Press.

Dow, Bonnie. 1996. *Prime-Time Feminism*. Philadelphia: University of Pennsylvania Press.

Doyle, Arthur. 1967. "The Final Problem." In *The Annotated Sherlock Holmes*, edited by William Baring-Gould, 2:301–18. New York: Clarkson N. Potter Publisher.

Dreier, Peter, and John Atlas. 2009. "*The Wire*—Bush-Era Fable about America's Urban Poor?" *City & Community* 8(3): 329–40.

Duff, Anthony, and David Garland. 1994. Introduction to *Punishment: A Reader*, edited by Anthony Duff and David Garland, 1–43. London: Oxford University Press.

Dunning, John. 1998. *On the Air: The Encyclopedia of Old-Time Radio*. New York: Oxford University Press.

Eaton, Mary. 1995. "A Fair Cop? Viewing the Effects of the Canteen Culture in *Prime Suspect* and *Between the Lines*." In *Crime and the Media: The Post-Modern Spectacle*, edited by David Kidd-Hewitt and Richard Osborne, 164–84. London: Pluto Press.

Elasmar, Michael, Kazumi Hasegawa, and Mary Brian. 1999. "The Portrayal of Women in U.S. Prime Television." *Journal of Broadcasting & Electronic Media* 44(1): 20–34.

Ericson, Richard, Patricia Baranek, and Janet Chan. 1991. *Representing Order: Crime, Law, and Justice in the News Media*. Toronto: University of Toronto Press.

Eschholz, Sarah, Ted Chiricos, and Marc Gertz. 2003. "Television and Fear of Crime: Program Types, Audience Traits and the Mediating Effect of Perceived Neighborhood Racial Composition." *Social Problems* 50:395–415.

Everhart, Karen. 2006. "Tennison Goes All the Way to the Bottom." *Current*, November 6.

Flett, Kathryn. 2003. "The Guv Is a Goddess." *Observer*, November 16. http://browse.guardian.co.uk/search/From+the+Observer?search=mirren+%26+goddes&sitesearch-radio=From%2Bthe%2BObserver.

Gardner, John. 1982. *On Moral Fiction*. New York: Basic Books.

Gaston, K., and J. Alexander. 1997. "Women in the Police: Factors Influencing Managerial Advancement." *Women in Management Review* 12:47–55.

Gilligan, Carol. 1982. *In a Different Voice*. Cambridge, MA: Harvard University Press.

Gilliam, Frank, and Shanto Iyengar. 2000. "Prime Suspects: The Influence of Local Television on the Viewing Public." *American Journal of Political Science* 44:560–73.

Gitlin, Todd. 1983. *Inside Prime Time*. New York: Pantheon.

Gledhill, Christine. 1988. "Pleasurable Negotiations." In *Female Spectators*, edited by Deidre Pribram, 64–89. New York: Verso Books.

Gordon, Avery. 1997. *Ghostly Matters: Haunting and the Sociological Imagination*. Minneapolis: University of Minnesota Press.

Grant, Judith. 1992. "Prime Time Crime: Television Portrayals of Law Enforcement." *Journal of American Culture* 15:57–68.

Gray, Herman. 1995. *Watching Race: Television and the Struggle for Blackness*. Minneapolis: University of Minnesota Press.

Griffith, Crystal. 2005. "Freedom Dreams: Cultivating a Cinema of Risk." Manuscript.

Hale, Beth. 2006. "Lynda La Plante's Fury over Alcoholic Final Act for *Prime Suspect*." *Mail Online*, October 20.

Hall, Stuart. 1979. "Culture, the Media, and Ideological Effect." In *Mass Communication and Society*, edited by J. Curran, M. Guervitch, and J. Woollacott, 315–48. Beverly Hills: Sage.

Hallam, Lynda. 2005. *Lynda La Plante*. Manchester: Manchester University Press.

Hammett, Dashiell. 1930. *The Maltese Falcon*. New York: Knopf.

Harrington, Ellen. 2007. "Nation, Identity and the Fascination with Forensic Science in Sherlock Holmes and CSI." *International Journal of Cultural Studies* 10(3): 365–82.

Haskell, Molly. 1974. *From Reverence to Rape: The Treatment of Women in the Movies*. New York: Holt, Rinehart and Winston.

Heidensohn, Frances. 1992. *Women in Control? The Role of Women in Law Enforcement*. New York: Oxford University Press.

Hirsch, Foster. 1981. *The Dark Side of the Screen: Film Noir*. San Diego: A. S. Barnes.

Hochschild, Arlie. 2009. "Through an Emotions Lens." In *Theorizing Emotions: Sociological Explorations and Applications*, edited by Debora Hopkins, Jochen Kleres, Helena Flam, and Helmut Kuzmics, 29–38. New York: Campus Verlag.

Holdaway, S., and S. Parker. 1998. "Policing Women Police: Uniform, Patrol, Promotion and Representation in the CID." *British Journal of Criminology* 38:40–60.

Human Rights Watch. 2001. "Bosnia: Landmark Verdicts for Rape, Torture, and Sexual Enslavement." http://www.hrw.org/english/doc/docs/2001/02/22/bosher256_ext.htm.

Hunt, Jennifer. 1990. "The Logic of Sexism among Police." *Women & Criminal Justice* 1:3–30.

Irons, Glenwood. 1995. "Introduction: Gender and Genre: The Woman Detective and the Diffusion of Generic Voices." In *Feminism in Women's Detective Fiction*, edited by Glenwood Irons, ix–xxiv. Toronto: University of Toronto Press.

Jermyn, Deborah. 2001. "Death of the Girl Next Door: Celebrity, Femininity and Tragedy in the Murder of Jill Dando." *Feminist Media Studies* 1:342–59.

———. 2003. "Women with a Mission: Lynda La Plante, DCI Jane Tennison and the Reconfiguration of TV Crime Drama." *International Journal of Cultural Studies* 6(1): 46–63.

———. 2004. "In Love with Sarah Jessica Parker: Celebrating Female Fandom and Friendship in *Sex and the City*." In *Reading "Sex and the City*," edited by Kim Akass and Janet McCabe, 201–18. London: I. B. Tauris.

———. 2010. *Prime Suspect*. London: Palgrave/Macmillan.

Jewkes, Yvonne. 2004. *Media & Crime*. London: Sage.

Johnston, Claire. 1999. "Women's Cinema as Counter-Cinema." In *Feminist Film Theory: A Reader*, edited by Sue Thornham, 31–40. New York: New York University Press.

Jones, S. 1986. *Policewomen and Equality*. London: Macmillan.

Josephson, Peter, and Rebecca Colton Josephson. 2009. "The Reformer and Her Work: Transgression, Alienation, and Feminine Identity in the Police Procedural." In *You've Come a Long Way, Baby: Women Politics and Popular Culture*, edited by Lilly J. Goren, 73–92. Lexington: University Press of Kentucky.

Jurik, Nancy. 1988. "Striking a Balance: Female Correctional Officers, Gender Role Stereotypes, and Male Prisons." *Sociological Inquiry* 58:291–305.

Jurik, Nancy, and Susan Martin. 2001. "Femininities, Masculinities and Organizational Conflict: Women in Criminal Justice Occupations." In *Women, Crime, and Criminal Justice*, edited by Claire Renzetti and Lynn Goodstein, 264–81. Los Angeles: Roxbury.

Kanter, Rosebeth. 1977. *Men and Women of the Corporation*. New York: Basic Books.

Kaplan, Cora. 1993. "Dirty Harriet/Blue Steel: Feminist Theory Goes to Hollywood." *Discourse* 16(1): 50–70.

Klein, Dorie. 1992. "Reading the New Feminist Mystery: The Female Detective, Crime and Violence." *Women & Criminal Justice* 4(1): 37–62.

Klein, Kathleen. 1995. *The Woman Detective: Gender & Crime*. 2nd ed. Chicago: University of Illinois Press.

Knight, Steven. 1980. *Form and Ideology in Crime Fiction*. Bloomington: Indiana University Press.

———. 2004. *Crime Fiction, 1800–2000: Detection, Death, Diversity*. London: Palgrave/Macmillan.

Krutnik, Frank. 1991. *In a Lonely Street: Film Noir, Genre, Masculinity*. London: Routledge.

Lakoff, George. 2006. *Thinking Points: Communicating Our American Values and Vision*. New York: Farrar, Straus and Giroux.

Lambert, Angela. 1993. "Interview/DCI Jane Tennison? Yes, That Was Me." *Independent*, June 15. http://www.independent.co.uk/life-style/interview—dci-jane-tennison-yes-that-was-me-prime-suspect-was-far-more-than-mere-tv-for-jackie-malton-on-whose-rebellious-career-helen-mirrens-detective-was-based-1491767.html.

La Plante, Lynda. 2001. *Above Suspicion*. New York: Touchstone.

Lenz, Timothy. 2003. *Changing Images of Law in Film and Television Crime Stories*. New York: Peter Lang.

Loader, Ian, and Aogan Mulcahy. 2003. *Policing and the Condition of England: Memory, Politics, and Culture*. Oxford: Oxford University Press.

Lotz, Amanda. 2001. "Postfeminist Television Criticism: Rehabilitating Critical Terms and Identifying Postfeminist Attributes." *Feminist Media Studies* 1(1): 105–21.

———. 2006. *Redesigning Women: Television after the Network Era*. Urbana: University of Illinois Press.

Luhr, William. 1991. *Raymond Chandler and Film*. 2nd ed. Tallahassee: Florida State University Press.

Luke, Cameron. 1993. "Media and Popular Culture in Education and Society: An Introduction to Education Studies." *Teaching Education* 5(2): 41–56.

Maltby, Richard. 1995. *Hollywood Cinema*. Cambridge: Basil Blackwell.

Mandel, Ernest. 1984. *Delightful Murder: A Social History of the Crime Story*. Minneapolis: University of Minnesota Press.

Martin, Susan. 1980. *Breaking and Entering: Policewomen on Patrol*. Berkeley: University of California Press.

Martin, Susan, and Nancy Jurik. 2007. *Doing Justice, Doing Gender: Women in Legal and Criminal Justice Occupations*. 2nd ed. Thousand Oaks, CA: Sage.

Mawby, Rob. 2003. "Completing the 'Half-Formed Picture'? Media Images of

Policing." In *Criminal Vision: Media Representation of Crime and Justice*, edited by Paul Mason, 214–35. London: Willan.

Mayer, Jane. 2007. "Whatever It Takes: The Politics of the Man behind '24.'" *New Yorker*, February 19–26, 66–80.

McCullagh, Ciarian. 2002. *Media Power: A Sociological Introduction*. New York: Palgrave.

McFerran, Ann. 2006. "Jackie Malton." *Sunday Times*, January 29. http://www.timesonline.co.uk/tol/life_and_style/article715415.ece.

McLaughlin, Eugene. 2005. "From Reel to Ideal: The Blue Lamp and the Popular Cultural Construction of the English 'Bobby.'" *Crime Media Culture* 1(1): 11–30.

McRobbie, Angela. 2007. "Postfeminism and Popular Culture: Bridget Jones and the New Gender Regime." In *Interrogating Postfeminism: Gender and the Politics of Culture*, edited by Yvonne Tasker and Diane Negra, 27–39. Durham, NC: Duke University Press.

Mellencamp, Patricia. 1995. *A Fine Romance: Five Ages of Feminism*. Philadelphia: Temple University Press.

Messerschmidt, James. 2000. *Nine Lives: Adolescent Masculinities, the Body and Violence*. Boulder, CO: Westview Press.

Miller, Susan, Kate Forest, and Nancy Jurik. 2004. "Lesbians in Policing: Perceptions and Work Experiences within the Macho Cop Culture." In *The Criminal Justice System and Women*, 3rd ed., edited by Barbara Price and Natalie Sokoloff, 511–26. New York: McGraw-Hill.

Mittell, Jason. 2004. *Genre and Television: From Cop Shows to Cartoons in American Culture*. New York: Routledge.

———. 2009. "Lost in a Great Story: Evaluation in Narrative Television [and Television Studies]." In *Reading "Lost": Perspectives on a Hit Television Show*, edited by Roberta Pearson, 119–38. London: I. B. Tauris.

Mizejewski, Linda. 2004. *Hardboiled & High Heeled: The Woman Detective in Popular Culture*. New York: Routledge.

Moore, Lori. 2010. "In the Life of 'The Wire.'" *New York Review of Books*, October 14. http://www.nybooks.com/articles/archives/2010/oct/14/life-wire/.

Morash, Merry, and Jack Greene. 1986. "Evaluating Women on Patrol: A Critique of Contemporary Wisdom." *Evaluation Review* 10:230–55.

Mosley, Walter. 1990. *Devil in a Blue Dress*. New York: Simon and Schuster.

Moyers, Bill, and David Simon. 2011. "The Straight Dope: Bill Moyers Interviews David Simon." *Guernica Magazine*. April. http://www.guernicamad.com/interviews/2530/simon_4_1_11/.

Munt, Sally. 1994. *Murder by the Book: Feminism and the Crime Novel*. London: Routledge.

Murphy, Jeffrie. 1973. "Marxism and Retribution." *Philosophy and Public Affairs* 2:217–43.

Naffine, Ngaire. 1997. *Feminism and Criminology*. London: Polity Press.

National Public Radio. 2010. "Power Player: Kyra Sedgwick Returns in *The Closer*." *Morning Edition*, July 12.

Nelsen, Robin. 1997. *TV Drama in Transition: Forms, Values and Cultural Change.* London: Macmillan.

Nunn, Heather, and Anita Biressi. 2003. "Silent Witness: Detection, Femininity, and the Post-Mortem Body." *Feminist Media Studies* 3(2): 193–206.

O'Connor, John. 1997. "Female Cop Has Attitude, Will Go Far." *New York Times*, February 7.

Oliver, Mary, and Blake Armstrong. 1998. "The Color of Crime: Perceptions of Caucasians' and African-Americans' Involvement in Crime." In *Entertaining Crime: Television Reality Programs*, edited by Mark Fishman and Gray Cavender, 19–36. New York: Aldine de Gruyter.

O'Sullivan, Sean. 2005. "UK Policing and Its Television Portrayal: 'Law and Order' Ideology or Modernising Agenda?" *Howard Journal* 44(5): 504–26.

Penfold-Mounce, Ruth, David Beer, and Roger Burrows. 2011. "*The Wire* as Social-Science Fiction?" *Sociology* 41(1): 152–67.

Perlmutter, David. 2000. *Policing the Media: Street Cops and Public Perceptions of Law Enforcement.* Thousand Oaks, CA: Sage.

Petit, Chris. 2008. "Non-Fiction Boy." *Guardian*, December 27. http://www.guardian.co.uk/culture/2008/dec/27/tv-drama-david-simon-wire-shield/print.

Press, Andrea. 1991. *Women Watching Television: Gender, Class, and Generation in the American Television Experience.* Philadelphia: University of Pennsylvania Press.

Prime Suspect 6 Production Notes. n.d. http://www.pbs.org/wgbh/masterpiece/primesuspect6/notes.html, accessed January 3, 2012.

Projansky, Sarah. 2001. *Watching Rape: Film and Television in Postfeminist Culture.* New York: New York University.

Rafter, Nicole. 2008. "Crime, Film and Criminology: Recent Sex-Crime Movies." *Theoretical Criminology* 11(9): 403–20.

Rapping, Elayne. 1992. *The Movie of the Week: Private Stories, Public Events.* Minneapolis: University of Minnesota Press.

———. 2003. *Law and Justice as Seen on TV.* New York: New York University Press.

Reddy, Maureen. 1988. *Sisters in Crime: Feminism and the Crime Novel.* New York: Continuum.

———. 2003. *Traces, Code, and Clues: Reading Race in Crime Fiction.* New Brunswick, NJ: Rutgers University Press.

Reiner, Robert. 1994. "The Dialectics of Dixon: The Changing Image of the TV Cop." In *Police Force, Police Service: Care and Control in Britain*, edited by Mike Stephens and Saul Becker, 11–31. Basingstoke: Macmillan.

Rennert, Amy. 1995. Introduction to *Helen Mirren: Prime Suspect*, edited by Amy Rennert, 12–13. San Francisco: KQED Books.

Reskin, Barbara, and Irene Padavic. 2002. *Men and Women at Work.* 2nd ed. Thousand Oaks, CA: Sage.

Rhodes, Jane. 1991. "Television's Realist Portrayal of African-American Women and the Case of *L.A. Law.*" *Women and Language* 15:424–29.

Roe, Dan, and Marti Cecilia Collins. 2009. "Power *Wire*: Understanding the Depiction of Power in TV Drama." *Journal of the Institute of Justice and International Studies* 9:182–92.

Rogers, Dave. 1989. *The Complete Avengers*. New York: St. Martin's Press.

Romero, Mary. 2001. "Teaching for Understanding Justice Studies: Moving beyond and against Students' Traditional Criminal Justice Perspective." Carnegie Scholars Program, Carnegie Academy for Scholarship of Teaching and Learning, Menlo Park, CA.

Savelsberg, Joachim. 1999. "Knowledge, Domination, and Criminal Punishment." *American Journal of Sociology* 99:911–43.

Scaggs, John. 2005. *Crime Fiction*. London: Routledge.

Schattenberg, Gus. 1981. "Social Control Functions of Mass Media Depictions of Crime." *Sociological Inquiry* 51:71–77.

Schulz, Dorothy. 1995. *From Social Worker to Crime Fighter: Women in United States Municipal Policing*. Westport, CT: Prager.

Scott, A. 1997. "Promotion in the Police Service: The Significance of Gender." PhD diss., University of Portsmouth.

Segal, Elizabeth. 2007. "Social Empathy: A New Paradigm to Address Poverty." *Journal of Poverty: Innovations on Social, Political and Economic Inequalities* 11:65–81.

Shales, Tom. 1995. "*Prime Suspect 3*." In *Helen Mirren: A Celebration of "Prime Suspect,"* edited by Amy Rennert, 64–70. San Francisco: KQED Books.

Silvestri, Marisa. 2003. *Women in Charge: Policing, Gender and Leadership*. Cullompton: Willan Publishing.

———. 2006. "Doing Time: Becoming a Police Leader." *International Journal of Police Science and Management* 8:266–81.

Smith, D., and J. Gray. 1985. *Police and People in London: A Survey of Londoners*. London: Policy Studies Institute.

Smith, Dorothy. 1979. "A Sociology for Women." In *The Prism of Sex: Essays in the Sociology of Knowledge*, edited by J. Sherman and E. Beck, 135–87. Madison: University of Wisconsin.

Smith, Sharon. 1999. "The Image of Women in Film: Some Suggestions for Future Research." In *Feminist Media Theory: A Reader*, edited by Sue Thornham, 14–19. New York: New York University Press.

Stanko, Elizabeth. 1985. *Intimate Intrusions*. London: Routledge and Kegan Paul.

Sydney-Smith, Susan. 2007. "Endless Interrogation: Prime Suspect Deconstructing Realism through the Female Body." *Feminist Media Studies* 7(2): 189–202.

———. 2009. "Buddies, Bitches, Broads: The British Female Cop Show." *Film International* 7(2): 46–58.

Tasker, Yvonne, and Diane Negra. 2007. "Introduction: Feminist Politics and Postfeminist Culture." In *Interrogating Postfeminism: Gender and the Politics of Culture*, edited by Yvonne Trasker and Diane Negra, 1–26. Durham, NC: Duke University Press.

Telegraph. 2009. "*The Wire*: Arguably the Greatest Television Programme Ever Made." April. http://www.telegraph.co.uk/news/uknews/5095500/.

Thompson, Jon. 1993. *Fiction, Crime and Empire: Clues to Modernity and Post-Modernism.* Urbana: University of Illinois Press.

Thornham, Sue. 1994. "Feminist Interventions: *Prime Suspect 1.*" *Critical Survey* 6(2): 226–33.

Tomc, Sandra. 1995. "Questing Women: The Feminist Mystery after Feminism." In *Feminism in Women's Detective Fiction,* edited by Glenwood Irons, 46–61. Toronto: University of Toronto Press.

Trier, James. 2007. "Teaching Theory through Popular Culture Texts." *Teaching Education* 18(2): 151–65.

Walkgate, Sandra. 1995. *Gender and Crime: An Introduction.* New York: Prentice Hall/Harvester Wheatsheaf.

Walkowitz, Judith. 1982. "The Myth of Male Violence." *Feminist Studies* 18(3): 542–74.

Walton, Priscilla, and Manina Jones. 1999. *Detective Agency: Women Rewriting the Hard-Boiled Tradition.* Berkeley: University of California Press.

Weisberg, Jacob. 2006. "*The Wire* on Fire." *Slate Magazine,* September 13. http://www.slate.com/id/214566/.

West, Candace, and Don Zimmerman. 1987. "Doing Gender." *Gender & Society* 1:125–51.

Westmarland, Louise. 2001. *Gender and Policing.* Devon: Willan Publishing.

Williams, Raymond. 1989. *On Television: Selected Writings.* London: Routledge.

Wilson, Christopher. 2000. *Cop Knowledge: Police Power and Cultural Narrative in Twentieth-Century America.* Chicago: University of Chicago Press.

———. 2005. "Let's Work Out the Details: Interrogation and Deception in Prime Time." *Journal of Criminal Justice and Popular Culture* 12(1): 47–64.

Wilson, William Julius. 1997. *When Work Disappears: The World of the New Urban Poor.* New York: Vintage.

Wittebols, James. 2004. *The Soap Opera Paradigm: Television Programming and Corporate Priorities.* Lanham, MD: Rowman & Littlefield Publishers.

Wykes, Maggie, and B. Gunter. 2005. *The Media and Body Image: If Looks Could Kill.* London: Sage.

Young, Iris. 1990. *Justice and the Politics of Difference.* Princeton, NJ: Princeton University Press.

———. 1994. "Punishment, Treatment, Empowerment: Three Approaches to Policy for Pregnant Addicts." *Feminist Studies* 20:33–55.

Index

GRAY CAVENDER is a professor of criminology in the School of Justice & Social Inquiry at Arizona State University.

NANCY C. JURIK is a professor of sociology and director of graduate studies in the School of Justice & Social Inquiry at Arizona State University.

The University of Illinois Press
is a founding member of the
Association of American University Presses.

———————————————

Composed in 10/13 Adobe Minion Pro
with Centaur MT display
by Barbara Evans
at the University of Illinois Press
Manufactured by Thomson-Shore, Inc.

University of Illinois Press
1325 South Oak Street
Champaign, IL 61820-6903
www.press.uillinois.edu